孫子兵法

VII

Position Perspective Opportunities Probability Mistakes Situations Momentum Rewards Vulnerabilities

Sun Tzu's
Art of War
Playbook
Volume 7 of 9:
Momentum

Gary
Gagliardi

Sun Tzu's
Art of War

Playbook

Volume Eight:
Rewards

by Gary Gagliardi
The Science of Strategy Institute
Clearbridge Publishing

Published by
Science of Strategy Institute, Clearbridge Publishing
suntzus.com scienceofstrategy.org

First Print Edition
Library of Congress Control Number: 2014909969
Also sold as an ebook under the title Sun Tzu's Warrior Rule Book
Copyright 2010, 2011, 2012, 2013, 2014 Gary Gagliardi
ISBN 978-1-929194-82-7(13-digit) 1-929194-82-x (10-digit)

Originally published as a series of articles on the Science of Strategy Website, scienceofstratregy.org. and
later as an ebook on various sites.

PO Box 33772, Seattle, WA 98133
Phone: (206)542-8947 Fax: (206)546-9756
beckyw@clearbridge.com
garyg@scienceofstrategy.org

Manufactured in the United States of America.
Interior and cover graphic design by Dana and Jeff Wincapaw.
Original Chinese calligraphy by Tsai Yung, Green Dragon Arts, www.greendragonarts.com.

Publisher's Cataloging-in-Publication Data
Sun-tzu, 6th cent. B.C.
Strategy, positioning, success, probability
    [Sun-tzu ping fa, English]
    Art of War Playbook / Sun Tzu and Gary Gagliardi.
    p.197 cm. 23
    Includes introduction to basic competitive philosophy of Sun Tzu

Clearbridge Publishing's books may be purchased for business, for any promotional use,
or for special sales.

Contents

Playbook Overview

Note: This overview is provided for those who have not read the previous volume of Sun Tzu's Art of War Playbook. *It provides an brief overview of the work in general and the general concepts framing the first volume.*

Sun Tzu's **The Art of War** is less a "book" in the modern Western sense than it is an outline for a course of study. Like Euclid's Geometry, simply reading the work teaches us very little. Sun Tzu wrote in in a tradition that expected each line and stanza to be studied in the context of previous statements to build up the foundation for understanding later statements.

To make this work easier for today's readers to understand, we developed the **Strategy Playbook**, the Science of Strategy Institute (SOSI) guidebook to explaining Sun Tzu's strategy in the more familiar format of a series of explanations with examples. These lessons are framed in the context of modern competition rather than ancient military warfare.

This Playbook is the culmination of over a decade of work breaking down Sun Tzu's principles into a series of step-by-step practical articles by the Institute's multiple award-winning author and founder, Gary Gagliardi. The original **Art of War** was written for military generals who understood the philosophical concepts of ancient China, which in itself is a practical hurdle that most modern readers cannot clear. Our **Art of War Playbook** is written for today's reader. It puts Sun Tzu's ideas into everyday, practical language.

The Playbook defines a new science of strategic competition aimed at today's challenges. This science of competition is designed as the complementary opposite of the management science that is taught in most business schools. This science starts, as Sun Tzu did himself, by defining a better, more complete vocabulary for discussing competitive situations. It connects the timeless ideas of Sun Tzu to today's latest thinking in business, mathematics, and psychology.

The entire Playbook consists of two hundred and thirty articles describing over two-thousand interconnected key methods. These articles are organized into nine different areas of strategic skill from understanding positioning to defending vulnerabilities. All together this makes up over a thousand pages of material.

Playbook Access

The Playbook's most up-to-date version is available as separate articles on our website. Live links make it easy to access the connections between various articles and concepts. If you become a SOSI Member, you can access any Playbook article at any time and access their links.

However, at the request of our customers, we also offer these articles as a series of nine <u>eBooks</u>. Each of the nine sections of the entire Playbook makes up a separate eBook, Playbook Parts One Through Nine. These parts flow logically through the Progress Cycle of listen-aim-move-claim (see illustration). Because of the dynamic nature of the on-line version, these eBooks are not going to be as current as the on-line version. You can see a outline of current Playbook articles here and, generally, the eBook version will contain most of the same material in the same order.

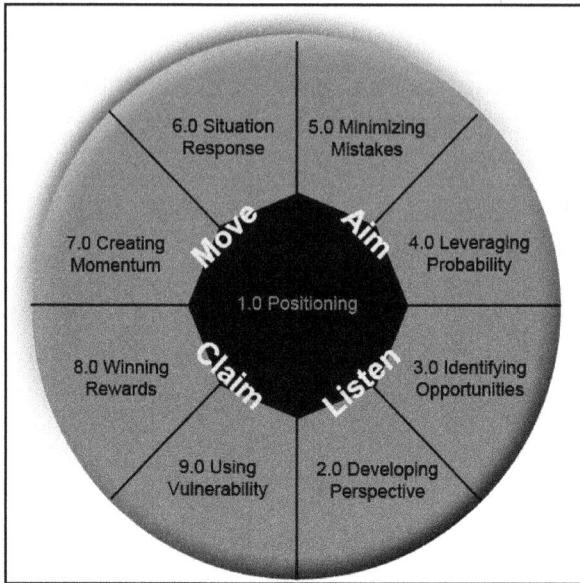

Nine categories of strategic skills define cycle that advances our positions:

1. Comparing Positions,

2. Developing Perspective,

3. Identifying Opportunities,

4. Leveraging Probability,

5. Minimizing Mistakes,

6. Responding To Situations,

7. Creating Momentum,

8. Winning Rewards, And

9. Defending Vulnerabilities.

Playbook Structure and Design

These articles are written in standard format including 1) the general principle, 2) the situation, 3) the opportunity, 4) the list of specific Art of War key methods breaking down the general principle into a series of actions, and 5) an illustration of the application of each of those key methods to a specific competitive situation. Key methods are written generically to apply to every competitive arena (business, personal life, career, sports, relationships, etc.) with each specific illustrations drawn from one of these areas.

A number identifies where each article appears in Playbook Structure. For example, the article 2.1.3 Strategic Deception is the third article in the first section of the second book in the nine volumes of the Strategy Playbook. In our on-line version, these links are live, clicking on them brings you to the article itself. We provide them because the interconnection of concepts is important in learning Sun Tzu's system.

Playbook Training

Training in Sun Tzu's warrior skills does not entail memorizing all these principles. Instead, these concepts are used to develop exercises and tools that allow trainees to put this ideas in practice. While each rule is useful, the heart of Sun Tzu system is the methods that connect all the principles together. Training in these principles is designed to develop a gut instinct for how Sun Tzu's strategy is used in different situations to produce success. Principles are interlinked because they describe a comprehensive conceptual mental model. Warrior Class training puts trainees in a situation where they must constantly make decisions, rewarding them for making decisions consist with winning productively instead of destructively.

About Positions

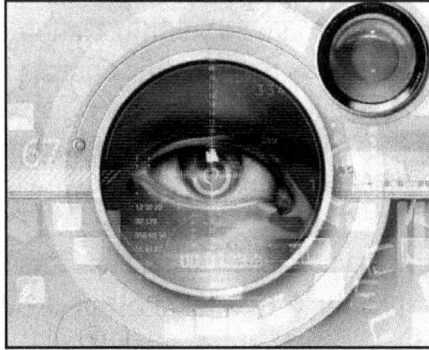

This first volume of Sun Tzu's Playbook focuses on teaching us the nature of strategic positions. "Position awareness" gives you a framework for understanding your strategic situation relative to the conditions around you. It enables you to see your position as part of a larger environment constructed of other positions and the raw elements that create positions. Master Sun Tzu's system of comparing positions, you can understand which aspect of your position are secure and which are the most dynamic and likely to change.

Traditional strategy defines a "position" as a comparison of situations. Game theory defines is as the current decision point that is arrive at as the sum or result of all previous decisions, both yours and those of others. Sun Tzu's methods of positioning awareness are different. They force you to see yourself in the eyes of others. Using these techniques, you broaden your perspective by gathering a range of viewpoints. In a limited sense, the scope of your position defines your area of control within your larger environment. In traditional strategy, five elements--mission, climate, ground, command, and methods--define the dimensions in which competitors can be compared.

Competition as Comparison

Sun Tzu saw that success is based on comparisons. This comparison must take place whenever a choice is made. For Sun Tzu, competition means a comparison of alternative choices or "positions". Battles are won by positioning before they are fought. These positions provide choices for everyone involved. Good positions discourage others from attacking you and invite them to support you. Sun Tzu's system teaches us how to systematically build up our positions to win success in the easiest way possible.

Competing positions are compared on the basis many elements, both objective and subjective. Sun Tzu's strategy is to identify these points of comparison and to understand how to leverage them. Learning Sun Tzu's strategy requires learning the details of how positions are compared and advanced. Sun Tzu taught that fighting to "sort things out" is a foolish way to find learn the strengths and weaknesses of a position. Conflict to tear down opposing positions is the most costly way to win competitive comparisons.

Today's More Competitive World

In the complex, chaotic world of today, we can easily get trapped into destructive rather than productive situations. Even our smallest decisions can have huge impact on our future. The problem is that we are trained for yesterday's world of workers, not today's world of warriors. We are trained in the linear thinking of planning in predictable, hierarchical world. This thinking applies less and less to today's networked, more competitive world.

Following a plan is the worker's skill of working in pre-defined functions in an internal, stable, controlled environment. The competitive strategy of Sun Tzu is the warrior's skill of making good decisions about conditions in complex, fast-changing, competitive environments. Sun Tzu's strategic system teaches us to adapt to the unexpected events that are becoming more and more common in our lives. We live in a world where fewer and fewer key events are planned. Navigating our new world of external challenges requires a different set of skills.

Most of us make our decisions without any understanding of competition. The result is that most of us lose as many battles as we win, never making consistent progress. Events buffet us, turning us in one direction and then the other. Too often, we end up repeating our past patterns of mistakes.

The Science of Strategy Institute teaches you the warrior's skills of adaptive response. There are many organizations that teach planning and organization. The Institute is one of the few places in the world you can get learn competitive thinking, and the only place in the world, with a comprehensive Playbook.

Seeing Situations Differently

Sun Tzu taught that a warrior's decision-making was a matter of reflex. As we develop our strategic decision-making skills, the critical conditions in situations simply "pop" out at us. This isn't magic. The latest research on how decisions are made tells us a lot about why Sun Tzu's principles work. It comes from using patterns to retrain our mind to see conditions differently. The study of successful response arose from military confrontations, where every battle clearly demonstrated how hard it is to predict events in the real world. Sun Tzu saw that winners were always those who knew how to respond appropriately to the dynamic nature of their situation.

Sun Tzu's principles provides a complete model for the key knowledge for understanding conditions in complex dynamic environments. This model "files" each piece of data into the appropriate place in the big picture. As the picture of your situation fills in, you can identify the opportunities hidden within your situation.

Making Decisions about Conditions

Instead of focusing on a series of planned steps, Sun Tzu's principles are about making decisions regarding conditions. It concerns itself with: 1) identifying the relative strengths and weaknesses of competitive positions, 2) advancing positions leveraging opportunities, and 3) the types of responses to specific challenges that work the most frequently. Using Sun Tzu's principles, we call these three areas position awareness , opportunity development , and situation response . Each area that we master broadens your capabilities.

- Position awareness trains us to recognize that competitive situations are defined by the relationship among alternative positions. Developing this perspective never ends. It deepens throughout our lives.
- Opportunity development explores the ground, testing our perceptions. Only testing the edges of perspective through action can we know what is true.
- Situation response trains us to recognize the key characteristics of the immediate situation and to respond appropriately. Only by practice, can we learn to trust the viewpoint we have developed.

Success in competitive environments comes from making better decisions every day. Sharp strategic reflexes flow from a clear understanding of where and when you use which competitive tools methods.

The Key Viewpoints

As an individual, you have a unique and valuable viewpoint, but every viewpoint is inherently limited by its own position. The result is that people cannot get a useful perspective on their own situations and surrounding opportunities. The first formula of positioning awareness involve learning what information is relevant. The most advanced techniques teach how to gather that information and put it into a bigger picture.

Most people see their current situations as the sum of their past successes and failures. Too often people dwell on their mistakes while simultaneously sitting on their laurels. Sun Tzu's strategy forces you to see your position differently. How you arrived at your current position doesn't matter. Your position is what it is. It is shaped by history but history is not destiny.

In this framework, the only thing that matters is where you are going and how you are going to get there. As you begin to develop your strategic reflexes, you start to think more and more about how to secure your current position and advance it.

Seeing the Big Picture

Most people see all the details of their lives, but they cannot see what those detail mean in terms of the big picture. As you master position awareness, you don't see your life as a point but as a path. You see your position in terms of what is changing and what resources are available. You are more aware of your ability to make decisions and your skills in working with others.

Most importantly, this strategic system forces you to get in touch with your core set of goals and values.

Untrained people usually see their life in terms of absolutes: successes and failures, good luck and bad, weakness and strength. As you begin to master position awareness, you begin to see all comparisons of strength and weakness are temporary and relative. A position is not strong or weak in itself. Its strength or weakness depends on how it compares or "fits" with surrounding positions. Weakness and strength are not what a position is, but how you use it.

The Power of Perspective

Positional awareness gives you the specialized vocabulary you need to understanding how situations develop. Mastering this vocabulary, you begin to see the leverage points connecting past and future. You replace vague conceptions of "strength," "momentum," and "innovation" with much more pragmatic definitions that you can actually use on a day to day basis.

Mastering position awareness also changes your relationships with other people. It teaches you a different way of judging truth and character. This methods allow you to spot self-deception and dishonest in others. It also allows you to understand how you can best work with others to compensate for your different weaknesses.

Once you develop a good perspective of position, it naturally leads you to want to learn more about how you can improve you position through the various aspects of opportunity development covered in the subsequent parts of the Strategy Playbook.

Seeing the Invisible

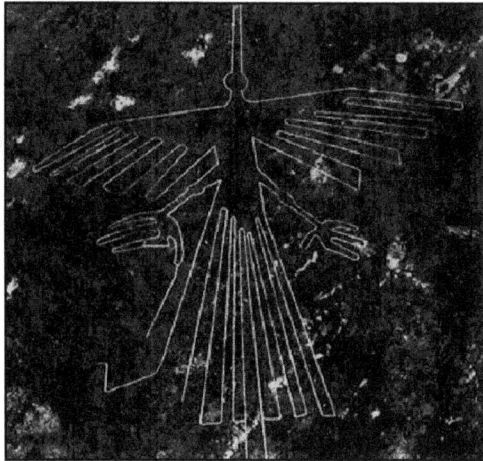

The "Nazca lines" are giant drawings etched across thirty miles of desert on Peru's southern coast. The patterns are only visible at a distance of hundreds of feet in the air. Below that, they look like strange paths or roads to nowhere. Just as we cannot see these lines without the proper perspective, people who master Sun Tzu's methods can suddenly recognize situations that were invisible to them before. Unless we have the right perspective, we cannot compare situations and positions successfully. The most recent scientific research explains why people cannot see these patterns for comparison without developing the network framework of adaptive thinking.[1]

Seeing Patterns

We can imagine patterns in chaotic situations, but seeing real pattern is the difference between success and failure. In our seminars, we demonstrate the power of seeing patterns in a number of exercises.

The mental models used by warrior give them "situation awareness." This situation awareness isn't just vague theory. Recent research shows that it can be measured in a variety of ways.[2] We now know that untrained people fall victim to a flow of confusing information because they don't know where its pieces fit. Those trained in Sun Tzu's mental models plug this stream of information quickly and easily into a bigger picture, transforming the skeleton's provided by Sun Tzu's system into a functioning awareness of your strategic position and its relation to other positions. Each piece of information has a place in that picture. As the information comes in, it fills in the picture, like pieces of a puzzle.

The ability to see the patterns in this bigger picture allows experts in strategy to see what is invisible to most people in a number of ways. They include:

- People trained in Art of War principles--<u>recognition-primed decision-making</u> --see patterns that others do not.
- Trained people can spot anomalies, things that should happen in the network of interactions but don't.
- Trained people are in touch with changes in the environment within appropriate time horizons.
- Trained people recognize complete patterns of interconnected elements under extreme time pressure.

Procedures Make Seeing Difficult

One of the most surprising discoveries from this research is that those who know procedures, that is, a linear view of events, alone have a ***more*** difficult time recognizing patterns than novices. An interesting study[3] examined the different recognition skills of three groups of people 1) experts, 2) novices, and 3) trainers who taught the standard procedures. The three groups were asked to pick out an expert from a group novices in a series of videos showing them performing a decision-making task, in this case, CPR. Experts were able to recognize the expert 90% of the time. Novices recognized the expert 50% of the time. The shocking fact was that trainers performed much worse that the novices, recognizing the expert only 30% of the time.

Why do those who know procedures fail to see what the experts usually see and even novices often see? Because, as research into <u>mental simulations</u> has shown, those with only a procedural model fit everything into that model and ignore elements that don't fit. In the above experiment, interviews with the trainers indicated that they assumed that the experts would always follow the procedural model. In real life, experts adapt to situations where unique conditions often trump procedure. Adapting to the situation rather than following set procedures is a central focus the form of strategy that the Institute teaches.

Missing Expected Elements

People trained to recognize the bigger picture beyond procedures also recognize when expected elements are missing from the picture. These anomalies or, what the cognition experts[4] describe as "negative cues" are invisible to novices *and* to those trained only in procedure. Without sense of the bigger pattern, people are focused too narrowly on the problem at hand. The "dog that didn't bark" from the Sherlock Holmes story, "Silver Blaze," is the most famous example of a negative cue. Only those working from a larger nonprocedural framework can expect certain things to happen and notice when they don't.

The ability to see what is missing also comes from the expectations generated by the mental model. Process-oriented models have the expectation of one step following another, but situation-recognition models create their expectations from signals in the environment. Research[5] into the time horizons of decision-makers shows that different time scales are at work. People at the highest level of organizations must look a year or two down the road, using strategic models that work in that timeframe, doing strategic planning. Decision-makers on the front-lines, however, have to react within minutes or even seconds to changes in their situation, working from their strategic reflexes. The biggest danger is that people get so wrapped up in a process that they lose contact with their environment.

Decisions Under Pressure

Extreme time pressure is what distinguishes front-line decision-making from strategic planners. One of the biggest discoveries in cognitive research[6] is that trained people do much better in seeing their situation instantly and making the correct decisions under time pressure. Researchers found virtually no difference between the decisions that experts made under time pressure when comparing them to decisions made without time pressure. That research also finds that those with less experience and training made dramatically worse decisions when they were put under time pressure.

The central argument for training our strategic reflexes is that our situation results, not from chance or luck, but from the instant decisions that that we all make every day. Our position is the sum of these decisions. If we cannot make the right decisions on the spot, when they are needed, our plans usually come to nothing. This is why we describe training people's strategic reflexes as helping them "do at first what most people only do at last."

The success people experience seeing what is invisible to others is dramatic. To learn more about how the strategic reflexes we teach differ from what can be planned, read about the contrast between planning and reflexes here . As our many members report, the success Sun Tzu's system makes possible is remarkable.

1 Chi, Glaser, & Farr, 1988, The Nature of Expertise, Erlbaum
2 Endsley & Garland, Analysis and Measurement of Situation Awareness
3 Klein & Klein, 1981, "Perceptual/Cognitive Analysis of proficient CPR Performance", Midwestern Psychological Association Meeting, Chicago.
4 Dr. David Noble, Evidence Based Research, Inc.In Gary Klein, Sources of Power, 1999
5 Jacobs & Jaques, 1991, "Executive Leadership".In Gal & Mangelsdofs (eds.), Handbook of Military Psychology, Wiley
6 Calder, Klein, Crandall,1988, "Time Pressure, Skill, and Move Quality in Chess". American Journal of Psychology, 101:481-493

About Creating Momentum

Adjusting to changing conditions advances a campaign only so far. The secret is knowing how to use innovation and surprise to create competitive momentum and excitement. That is the focus of the concepts in this volume of Sun Tzu's Playbook. The principles here teach you to use momentum to win new positions and grow your resources. Creating excitement from innovation is not that difficult.

Innovation is never in limited supply. Sun Tzu puts it this way:

> *You must use surprise for a successful invasion.*
> *Surprise is as infinite as the weather and land.*
> *Surprise is as inexhaustible as the flow of a river.*
>
> The Art of War, 5:2:4-7

Momentum combines what people expect with what they don't expect. Momentum comes from setting up pleasant surprises and timing those surprises to win positions.

The Chaos of the Marketplace

Sun Tzu's principles teach us that competition is never neat and tidy. We all want to work through a neat to-do list when sitting at our desk in our little protected environment. This isn't how success works.

Success comes from momentum. Momentum comes from balancing two opposite forces—organization and innovation—against one another.

People are confused by the chaos and disorder in any competitive situation. People cannot know what they want because they do not know what they can get. This confusion requires you to be organized. You must create orderly procedures and systems. All organizations must create islands of order amid the competitive chaos. Human uncertainty is thereby turned into confidence. Satisfying peoples' expectations gives you credibility in your competitive arena.

However, there is a limit to what you can gain this way.

Predictability is boring. People like visiting islands of order, but people don't like being confined to islands of order. Eventually they grow tired of the islands they know and stop visiting them. This is what creates new opportunities. People crave new experiences, but, at the same time, they fear the unknown. People appreciate high standards, but standards are eventually taken for granted. The world is changing so fast because people always want more and are always looking for new experiences.

Well-run organizations are not necessarily successful organizations. Successful organizations need something more to establish dominance over their competition.

Establish Standards to Create Order

The first principles in this volume define the need for standards and order. You must understand how people experience your competitive position. They are always comparing you to your competitors. You must organize what is confusing. When they visit your island of order in the confusing sea of the competition, they must know what to expect. To create a satisfying experience, you need to establish quality standards. You must use systems that have proven to be dependable.

Once they know you, people want consistency. They need predictability. You can't help that the world is chaotic, but you can eliminate any uncertainty within your operations. You create expectations and must know how to satisfy them.

You cannot make a profit and use resource efficiently without standard procedures. Chaos isn't profitable. It wastes time, effort, and resources. Organizing saves time, effort, and resources. This is where planning works. You perfect systems, practice procedures, train people, eliminate mistakes, and tighten up operations.

Good organizations create order to get value out of their resources. Great organizations create order to better satisfy other people to get value out of their resources. You cannot undermine how people experience your position. People must understand the basics of what you offer. Make it easy for people to work with you. They don't want to work to work with you. You must provide consistency quickly, with a minimum of effort.

Create Realistic Expectations

You cannot base your position simply on being different. You establish quality standards to set the expectations of others. You then use surprise to win them over. When you use surprise at the wrong time, people see you as a nut. Nuts get attention, but they don't win supporters. People cross the street to avoid a nut because nuts are just too unpredictable.

Before you can surprise people, they need expectations about who you are and what you offer. They must know that you aren't just a nut. Even in crowded competitive conditions, it is a mistaken to think that you first have to get people's attention.

The context can teach people to expect "a surprise." For example, if you are watching the Super Bowl, a crazy commercial cannot surprise you. Everyone expects loony commercials during the Super Bowl, and everyone also know that those commercials cost millions. They aren't really nuts. Of course, because you are expecting it, a crazy Super Bowl commercial isn't a surprise either.

For a surprise to work, the context has to frame your position correctly. When I give a keynote speech on strategy at a convention, I always start my presentation with something that the audience doesn't expect. Surprise works because their expectations have already been set. They know I am not a nut because the organization is paying several thousand dollars for me to talk to them.

An innovation cannot create a dominant position unless it is built on a solid foundation. Standards come first. The latest new electronic gadget is designed according to set standards, made mostly of proven components, built in factories by systems, and marketed and distributed by well-established procedures. For something "new" to work, it has to have a lot of old in it.

People can't relate to concepts that are too new. Personal computers didn't catch on until software makers realized that they needed to put more "old" into them. There were hundreds of calculating programs for personal computers before the first "electronic spreadsheet" was introduced. The fact that the electronic spreadsheet was modeled after something old, the standard accounting spreadsheet, was the key to its success, and, to a large degree, the whole success of the personal computer itself.

The simplest application of Sun Tzu's principles for creating momentum is to combine old and new product ideas together into a single package. The old idea part of the formula provides the context. This is a standard that people can understand. It creates their expectations. The new part is the surprise. It gets their attention and stimulates them with something new.

Rearrange Existing Components

Sun Tzu's system puts a big burden on creativity. You must plan some type of innovation every time you start a new campaign. You use the nature of your opportunity, your opportunity space, and the stage of the campaign to guide your choice of innovations. If you don't use surprise and innovation, your competitors will. Innovation harnesses the flow of change in the business environment to your benefit.

Where do you get these creative ideas? As always, today's problems are the seeds for tomorrow's inspiration. You always use your time to think of ways to improve your products and systems. If you think about the components of products and processes, you will come up with new ways to arrange them to create surprise and momentum.

Rearranging parts is the key. Just think about what the parts are, how they can be rearranged, and the implications of making changes. You just break everything down into its components and rearrange those components. In sales and marketing, there are only a few basic messages for selling products. In manufacturing, there are only a few key components to any product. In operations, there are only a few basic steps in any business processes. Just mix them up in your mind and see what happens.

What was the process of buying a cup of coffee before the half decaf, low fat venti mocha latte? How did Starbucks change it to create a dominant position? Coffee was one size fits all, but Starbucks added a million options. Now, you give your order to a clerk. The clerk writes it on a cup, repeats it the way you should have said it, and passes it to the coffee maker—barrista, if you prefer. I find this process annoying because, when the clerk repeats the order, I feel like I am being corrected for not using the official coffee terminology and proper word order.

How could you reinvent the process that Starbucks reinvented? Just rearrange things a little. Let your customers grab the size of cup they want, check off the little boxes themselves, and pass it to the coffee person. Voilà! No need to worry about terminology! No corrections! No mistakes!

You may not think you are creative, but you can always just rearrange things. Rearrange messages for marketing. Rearrange parts for new products. Rearrange steps for new processes. Just by rearranging, you come up with a new perspective. Do customers usually pay at the end of the process? How could they pay at the beginning? Starbucks moved paying to the middle.

Not all new ideas will work at first, but you can learn from your mistakes. It takes time to get innovations working. Frequently, the reason your innovation didn't work is that you didn't include enough "old" in your formula. Standards come first. Proven ideas that meet people's expectations are always the major ingredient. Innovation and proven practices are mutually dependent on each other. Standards inspire creativity, which inspires new standards. Using both, you can continually improve your business.

Without first establishing a baseline of standards, innovation and surprise are just chaos and confusion. Without innovation, standards are boring and just fall behind a marketplace that is constantly moving forward. You must combine standards with surprises to make the leap into a dominant position.

It is the addition of surprise to a solid position that creates the momentum toward a dominant position. Momentum never comes from consistency alone. The sense of momentum is created by a surprise—changes that get attention.

To offer a sports analogy, a team that is expected to win doesn't develop any momentum by scoring. Everyone expects the dominant team to score. Everyone expects the dominant team to be ahead in the game. When is momentum created? When something surprising happens in the game. This momentum is psychological and real. When expectations are exceeded, abilities are enhanced. When expectations are disappointed, abilities decline. A surprise opens up entirely new possibilities.

How many times have we witnessed this in sports? The underdog scores and momentum changes. Suddenly the favorite can't do anything right and the underdog can't make a mistake. Unless something else surprising happens, momentum doesn't change. The favorite can score, but momentum is still against them. They have to score in a surprising way, doing something that they don't normally do, for momentum to shift again.

You cannot control the chaos of your competitive environment. You can, however, control your momentum. You can do something surprising to change the situation. The change puts your competitors on the defensive. When you get momentum on your side, your competitors have to copy you. You can move from one innovation to another, abandoning them when they are no longer surprising. You can keep opponents following behind you. You don't have to worry as much about competitors when competitors are worrying about you. Your momentum with supporters forces competitors to keep up.

Time Innovation for Maximum Advantage

Together, the shift between standards and surprise creates momentum toward a dominant position, but timing is critical in securing that position. The chaos of competition is your target. You want changes to have an impact on the market. You can defuse the power of innovation by releasing changes at the wrong time or in the wrong way. Bundle small changes together to give them weight. Save up changes to release them to leverage.

The constant creativity of innovation, if hidden, builds up pressure. Timing reveals those surprises, releasing that pressure at the right time. Timing introduces a critical amount of control into the chaos of battle. It is this control that does the most to affect competitive attitudes.

You cannot release changes too soon, but you also cannot go too long without making changes. One step should follow another quickly. This type of continual progress can wash away any obstacles in a business and frustrate your competitors. This is the power of momentum.

Time surprises to impact those you want to influence. People's decisions take place in an instant. You must make an impact to win their support. Prepare your surprises for people in advance but keep them a secret. Release them at the right time to get the decisions that you want. This requires timing.

You must invest only in efforts that win supporters for your position. The shift from standards to surprise must have an impact. You must time your surprises precisely. A change from what is expected creates tension. You must time your surprise to create excitement among other people.

From the viewpoint of potential supporters, the excitement of change gives them the emotional impetus to make a decision. From the competitors' viewpoint, releasing an innovation at the right time increases their confusion and decreases their confidence. Even a small change from expectations can be enough to tip the balance if it is introduced at the right time.

The world of competition is chaotic and confusing. You create expectations to give people the sense that they are in control. You create pleasant surprises to stimulate people and to control them. These same surprises give your opponents the sense that you are in control. Since you and your people are more prepared for the change than others, especially your competitors are, you do attain more control the over chaos of the competition than your competitors do.

If competitors have a sense that you are in control, you have secured a dominant position. If they panic, they will make mistakes. These mistakes create new opportunities to advance.

You create a dominant position for momentum. You do not create it by asking yourself or your people to work harder. You must innovate the ways you handle the way people experience interactions with your position. You shape people's expectations to move them. People move forward when they know what to expect. Make people comfortable and they will support you. You use surprise to challenge them to act in a new way. Give people a sense of belonging and they will stay with you. Bring people together and they will move forward.

You use momentum to control people's thinking. You use people's thinking to control competitors. You want to shape the process so both your supporters and your competitors rush forward without stopping.

Summary

The principles in Volume Seven teach us how to give people a refuge from the chaotic world of competition by using standards that produce a consistent result. Start by giving people clear expectations about what they will get from dealing with you and satisfy those expectations.

These principles then explain how people get bored with having their expectations met. Give them something new and exciting in the way that you operate. They will keep coming back for more.

Finally, these principles teach you how to time your surprises to win supporters. Force your competitors to continually play catch-up. Give your competitors the sense that you are in control of chaos. They will continually feel at a disadvantage. This will pressure them into making mistakes. Their mistakes will open new opportunities for you.

7.0.0 Creating Momentum

Sun Tzu's seven key methods on how momentum requires creativity.

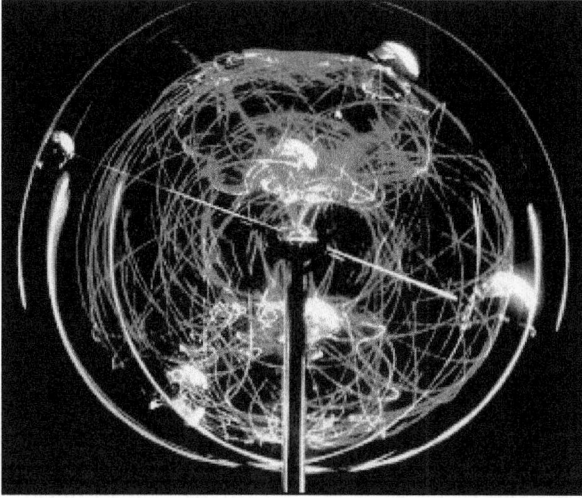

"You must develop these instant reflexes."
Sun Tzu's The Art of War 11:3:3

"When a warrior learns to stop the internal dialogue, everything becomes possible; the most far-fetched schemes become attainable. "
Carlos Castaneda

General Principle: We must drill ourselves to instantly recognize and respond to situations automatically.

Situation:

When we move to pursue an opportunity, we cross a critical threshold from simple decision-making to executing decisions. Sun Tzu called this movement "armed march" but we understand it more broadly as a competitive move or action. To pursue an opportunity, we must move into a region outside of our control. Once outside of controlled areas, we must respond instantly to the situations that we encounter. As important as reaction time is quickly deciding how to pursue opportunities, it is many times more important in responding to the immediate situations in which we find ourselves. Our range of potential actions collapses because the situation limits our options. If we don't know the best responses to these situations, we are going to get into serious trouble.

Opportunity:

Starting this new section, we move our discussion to the Move skills of Sun Tzu's Progress Cycle (1.8 Progress Cycle). Aim skills choose the highest probability opportunities (4.0 Leveraging Probability) and the best actions to explore them (5.0 Minimizing Mistakes). Move skills execute our aim decisions. Sun Tzu described in detail how they do this through situations response. These responses are required by situations that arise in the course of our move. There are nine classes of competitive situations that we encounter. Each of these classes has one best response. It gets even easier. While any of these classes of situations can arise in any move, they are most commonly found at certain stages of a competitive campaign.

Key Methods:

The following key methods guide the way that we respond to situation.

1. We must train ourselves to instantly recognize our situation. At this stage, the emphasis shifts from thought to action, from decision to execution. Our actions in a competitive environment are not executed like the steps in a plan. The job of making good strategic decisions gets more intense and demanding. We get information more quickly and we have to respond to it much more quickly as well (6.1 Situation Recognition).

2. We must also distinguish between simple moves and moves as a part of a larger campaign. A *campaign* describes longer term changes in position that consists of a sequence of moves. Campaigns are executed in smaller actions since smaller steps are more powerful. Within a campaign, we can recognize situations more easily because campaigns and the situations within them develop in a predictable, logical way (6.2 Campaigns).

3. Campaigns usually go through three stages. Each stage reveals more about the nature of the opportunity and has certain implications as far as creating situations. Understanding the stage of our campaign helps us better recognize the situation in which we find ourselves. Campaigns have beginning, middle, and end stages. Situations in each stage proceed logically from the nature of that stage (6.3 Campaign Patterns).

4. We must instantly separate competitive situations into one of the nine common classes. While every competitive situation has its unique characteristics, most fall into one of these nine categories. These nine situation classes are defined by differences in: 1) the true nature of the opportunity, 2) our position versus that of potential rivals, and 3) the depth of our commitment to the move (6.4 Nine Situations).

5. Once we recognize a situation, we must immediately know the one and only correct response. To reflect the fast pace of decision-making in making competitive moves, the best decisions are *responses* that arise from reflex rather than contemplation. Experience has demonstrated there is one, best response that works a high percentage of the time in each of the common situation. These responses have been proven over thousands of years of experience since they were first developed by Sun Tzu (6.5 Nine Responses).

6. We must pause our campaign when we run low on responses. The nine common situation responses are triggered by external developments. A growing lack of resources is an internal state that must also be monitored. While situation response requires us to focus externally on our situation, we cannot let ourselves lose sight of our internal need for resources (6.6 Campaign Pause).

7. Our dominant response must be tailored to three categories of unique characteristics. This is where the unique aspects of a position come into play. While our dominant response is dictated by standard situations, these same situations arise over and over again but they are never exactly the same. Every occurrence involves a unique constellation of conditions. We look at three categories of arena, relative size, and strength conditions *(*6.7 Special Conditions of Opposition).

8. Instant situation response creates key psychological advantages. By responding quickly and appropriately to challenging situations, we create confidence in our supporters and fear in our rivals. We improve the subjective dimensions of our position regardless of the objective rewards of our moves (6.8 Competitive Psychology).

Illustration:

The illustration that we usually use in our seminars to demonstrate these key aspects of situation response is a simple one of driving to the store to buy groceries. The decision that getting groceries is the best use of our time and that we are going to use a car are behind us. What happens when we get out on the road? This illustration makes solving these problems seem simple and indeed they are once we can apply them to every area of our competitive life as naturally as we do driving to the store.

1. We must train ourselves to instantly recognize our situation. If we don't run into problems, no responses are necessary. On this particular trip, we are going to run into problems. No strategic knowledge is necessary if we don't face challenges in our move. These principles are for meeting challenges.

2. We must also distinguish between simple moves and moves as a part of a larger campaign. Let us assume that getting bread is part of a larger campaign of making special dinner for guests, which has certain deadlines.

3. Campaigns usually go through three stages. This is an early stage of a campaign, so we expect three potential situations and prepare mentally for them.

4. We must instantly separate competitive situations into one of the nine common classes. An early stage has three possibilities and let us assume we hit them all. An intrusion threatens to interrupt us before we get out the door. We initially find no problems on the road. Then we hit a serious traffic jam.

5. *Once we recognize a situation, we must immediately know the one and only correct response.* We must know to 1) evade the intruder, 2) not get distracted and go quickly on the open road, and 3) know how to get around the traffic.

6. *We must pause our campaign when we run low on responses*. Running low on gas after getting out the door? Don't ignore it and hope you don't hit more problems. We'll be in a world of hurt when we hit traffic. We stop and get gas.

7. *Our dominant response must be tailored to three categories of unique characteristics.* We have to adjust our responses depending on how far it is to the store, how big the traffic jam, and road conditions. For example, if the road is icy and slippery, we don't choose the same alternatives as we do when the roads are bare and dry.

8. *Instant situation response creates key psychological advantages*. By navigating the challenging road conditions, we become come confident that our dinner party will go well.

7.1.0 Order from Chaos

Sun Tzu's seven key methods teaching the value of chaos in creating competitive momentum.

⚠ CAUTION

CHAOS FIELD
ESTIMATED STRENGTH: 47 KrZ

LIMIT EXPOSURE TO THIS AREA
AND REPORT ABNORMALITIES
IN YOUR LIFE AFTER EXPOSURE

"War is very complicated and confusing.
Battle is chaotic.
Nevertheless, you must not allow chaos."
Sun Tzu's The Art of War 5:4:1-3

"Chaos in the world brings uneasiness, but it also allows
the opportunity for creativity and growth."
Tom Barrett

General Principle: Only momentum from creativity can break through the chaos of competition.

Situation:

Chaos describes our inability to see a pattern. Order may exist in situations that appear chaotic, but we cannot see their order. Dynamic natural systems evolve in complexity until we can no longer see any underlying order. In a psychological sense, chaos is the cognitive dissonance that arises from reality failing to match our expectations. We are wired to find patterns even in meaningless noise. As patterns dissolve in the overwhelming complexity of a situation, we perceive chaos even as we cling to our original expectations. This conflict between what we see and what we expect creates confusion, frustration, and fear.

Opportunity:

We experience chaos in competitive events, but so does everyone else. We can use the uncertainty in chaotic environments to our advantage (2.1.2 Leveraging Uncertainty). Success is never neat and tidy. We can work through a neat to-do list while sitting at our desks, but this isn't how we create success in the larger world. Real success comes from getting in the middle of messy, chaotic situations and exploring their potential.

Key Methods:

The following key methods describe how we need to think about using chaos in competitive situations.

1. We use proven mental models to create some order in chaos. Our confusion creates the desire for predictability. Sun Tzu's science of strategy provides certain standard methods for responding to common situations. In using these responses, we earn the respect of others. In advancing our position, we capture territory and create islands of control amid the competitive chaos. Those who create order, get the support of those who want to escape from competitive chaos to an island of order (6.8 Competitive Psychology).

2. As order increases from proven responses, it creates the need for more chaos. Order and chaos are complementary opposites, balancing against each other. As a competitive arena becomes more controlled, the value of introducing more chaos increases. This is true even in our use of Sun Tzu's standard responses. Over time, people adapt to these responses. Some copy what we have been doing. Others prepare against us. We become predictable. As environments become more predictable, they become more boring. We yearn for novelty. Our proven standard responses make less and less progress (3.2.3 Complementary Opposites).

3. As our environment or methods grow more ordered, unexpected methods start working better. In a sense, we must stop making sense, at least in the same ways everyone else does. The need for novelty is a special form of the openings on which all strategic moves are based, but this opening comes from the expectations created by our own use of standards. Given that others have expectations of us, we can go beyond them. We can invent new moves that increase the natural chaos. We can make the most of an opportunity only by surprising others (3.1.4 Openings).

4. We can select unexpected, unproven methods that have a high-probability success. Sun Tzu's methods of using standards as the basis for innovations increases the likelihood that these unproven methods work. Proven methods might work better, except they don't because they are expected. If we add a pinch of innovation to a proven formula, the new formula will sometimes fail, but it will usually work, at least to some degree (7.1.3 Standards and Innovation).

5. The use of unproven methods always gives us the advantage of surprise. Our use of innovation is primarily designed to increase chaos in the situation. This is different than natural chaos in one key respect: we are prepared for it while others are not. The confusion, uncertainty, and fear arising naturally from chaos does not affect us in the same way that it affects others, giving us an advantage (7.1.2 Momentum Psychology).

6. Only by using unproven methods can we discover new methods that work better than proven methods. We cannot depend on this, but we cannot discount it either. Every innovation is an exploration of possibilities. Only through that exploration is discovery possible. Only new methods can reveal the emergent properties in the chaotic environment, which are the source of completely new forms of order. This discovery of new, previously unknown resources, are the basis of our large leaps forward in position (7.6.1 Resource Discovery).

7. Our discovery of new methods, opens up entirely new realms of chaos. Using Sun Tzu's methods, we can create surprises in a systematic way, but the results of some of that innovation are only predictable in limited ways. We always get the advantage of the temporary surprise. We occasionally, get the additional advantage of discovering a better method. Rarely, we also get the advantage of discovering new areas of chaos that we can tame (7.3 Strategic Innovation).

Illustration:

Let us illustrate these ideas by exploring the history of television.

1. We use proven mental models to create some order in chaos. At first, television was a media that no one knew how to use. There was no clear idea of schedules, formats, or even a clear separation between the shows and their commercials. The first television shows were simply video broadcasts of shows that had been popular on radio or in vaudeville in which the commercial sponsors played a dominant role.

2. As order increases from proven responses, it creates the need for more chaos. These early television shows became more predictable. Commercials became standardized. The most popular shows, such as the vaudeville of Milton Berle quickly became boring and fell out of popularity.

3. As our environment or methods grow more ordered, unexpected methods start working better. A wider variety of television shows began to appear, inventing new forms such as the sit-com with "I Love Lucy" (1951).

4. We can select unexpected, unproven methods that have a high-probability success. While new shows were developed for television, they used the same organization and dramatic structures that had been proven earlier in radio broadcasting. Most shows are inherently derivative, simply adding a set of new personalities to a proven format: sit-com, crime drama, medical drama, etc.

5. The use of unproven methods always gives us the advantage of surprise. The most popular shows are those that provide something unique. The Tonight Show breaks new ground as a late night format, starting in 1954 with Steve Allen. Bonanza is the first color series. Archie Bunker brought in contemporary values. The Simpsons was the first cartoon show for adults.

6. Only by using unproven methods can we discover new methods that work better than proven methods. While most television formats had their roots firmly in the past, certain new formats, such as the reality series, were completely new to the medium. Because of their economic advantages, such shows may be the dominant form of programming.

7. Our discovery of new methods, opens up entirely new realms of chaos. There are now so many television shows available that we need technologies from DVRs such as TIVO to help organize it.

7.1.1 Creating Surprise

Sun Tzu's five key methods for creating surprise using our chaotic environment.

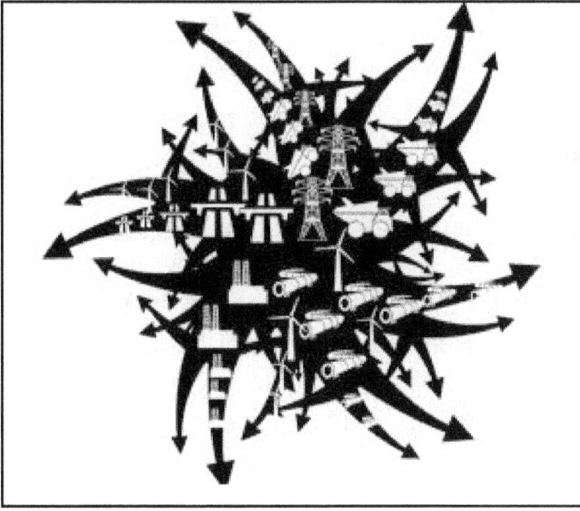

"You fight with momentum.
There are only a few types of surprises and direct
actions."

Sun Tzu's The Art of War 5:2:20-21

"Apprehension, uncertainty, waiting, expectation, fear of
surprise, do a patient more harm than any exertion."

Florence Nightingale

General Principle: Surprise requires chaos, expectations, and an unambiguous, intentional action.

Situation:

Though competition is inherently chaotic, we still expect it to make sense. We are wired to find patterns even in meaningless

noise. Despite the overwhelming complexity of competitive environments, we still cling to our expectations of order. Admitting
that we cannot understand a situation creates cognitive dissonance,
especially since we have been trained in linear thinking rather the
than adaptive methods of Sun Tzu's strategy. We cling to our expectation. We are surprised when situations fail to develop according
to those expectations. The reality of chaos affects us emotionally on
a subconscious level. The unrecognized chaos makes us feel tense,
frustrated, and even fearful.

Opportunity:

Our reaction to chaos makes surprise possible. When we use
surprise, we take advantage of the inherent chaos of the situation.
Since people are looking for patterns, they shift their focus to us. As
the author of a surprise, we are different from everyone else in the
situation. We alone are assumed to be in control of the event, and,
by proxy, of the situation. This changes the expectations of everyone with whom we deal. They grant us power over a situation that
everyone else sees as outside of their control. Everyone gauges their
reactions based upon that perception of power.

Key Methods:

We create surprise using the following five key methods.

*1. We leverage people's sense of expectations in a chaotic situ-
ation.* Chaos is a necessary ingredient to creating surprise. Competition is chaos, but we fool ourselves into thinking it is controlled.
Chaos creates a secret unease within us. Despite the rising feeling
of uncertainty created by competition, expectations about the future
are also necessary to create surprise. We can only be surprised if
we think we know what is happening and how events should unfold.
This means that the chaos cannot be so great that all expectations
get thrown out the window. An action must have expectations to
work against for it to be surprising (7.1.3 Standards and Innovation).

*2. We must use a set-up action that seems to violate expecta-
tions while secretly satisfying them.* We need to take an action that

violates apparent expectations but which really satisfies those who are expecting a surprise. In competitive situations, we only pretend to know what to expect. Deep down, we know they are chaotic. The set-up satisfies our secret expectation of the unexpected. However, it creates a deeper tension, as opponents try to respond to the set-up action correctly (2.0 Developing Perspective).

3. We must then use a follow-up action to create the surprise that gives us momentum. The setup is the unexpected for which others are prepared. It is the follow-up that creates surprise and from it, momentum. The unexpected puts others off-balance, but the surprise pushes them over. When we witness an event that violates our expectations, we start to worry about what we are missing. If the set-up was an accident, it has no meaning. We don't have to worry about it. The follow-up action proves that the set-up was intentional. The follow-up demonstrates our control over the situation, giving us the desired momentum (3.6 Leveraging Subjectivity).

4. Both set-up and its follow-up must be significant enough to force attention. If either action is minor, we will either overlook it or simply take the action in stride, without reassessing the situation. However, if the action is significant, we react differently. We cannot take it in stride because of its impact on our perceptions of the situation. We are forced to reassess the situation as a whole. Our new perception of the situation centers around the surprising event (2.3.1 Action and Reaction).

5. Both set-up and its follow-up must appear suddenly out of secrecy. This is a matter of good timing. Under the subtle tensions of a secretly chaotic situation, our first reaction is to fit all actions within our expected narrative. If the action can be interpreted as something expected, it will be interpreted as something expected, no matter how mistakenly. This can actually help us in early stages of preparing a surprise because it enables us to disguise the "set-up" as something familiar. If we use the action too soon or too late, it will lose most of its impact (7.4 Competitive Timing).

Illustration:

We can illustrate these ideas by using the way that a magic trick is constructed.

1. We leverage people's sense of expectations about a chaotic situation. The first part of a magic trick is called "The Pledge". The magician shows you something ordinary: a deck of cards, a bird or a man. He shows you this object. Perhaps he asks you to inspect it to see if it is indeed real, unaltered, normal. However, underlying the Pledge of ordinariness is the sense of something coming, a hidden secret, the beginning of tension.

2. We must use a set-up action that seems to violate expectations while secretly satisfying them. The second part of a magic trick is called "The Turn". The magician takes the ordinary something and makes it do something extraordinary. However, while the Turn seems extraordinary, it is really expected because people are watching a magic act.

3. We must then use a follow-up action to create the surprise that gives us momentum. This is the third part, called the Prestige. Making something disappear isn't enough; you have to bring it back. The Turn was expected, almost promised by the Pledge. It is the Prestige that finalizes the surprise, making us realize that the Turn was itself another Pledge.

4. Both set-up and the follow-up must be significant enough to force attention. Neither the Turn nor Prestige can be subtle. They must command our attention. They force us to figure out what is really going on. Together, they reinforce our attention. At first we were looking for a secret, but before we could resolve that quest, we are confronted with another. We won't find the secret, because we know we are looking in the wrong place.

5. Both the set-up and the follow-up must appear suddenly out of secrecy. Both the Turn and Prestige must happen suddenly, ideally when we aren't expecting it. Since we are expecting something from the Pledge, but the Turn relieves those expectations only to be confronted with the Prestige, this sudden revelation that causes us to recognize control.

7.1.2 Momentum Psychology

Sun Tzu's five key methods on the psychology of surprise.

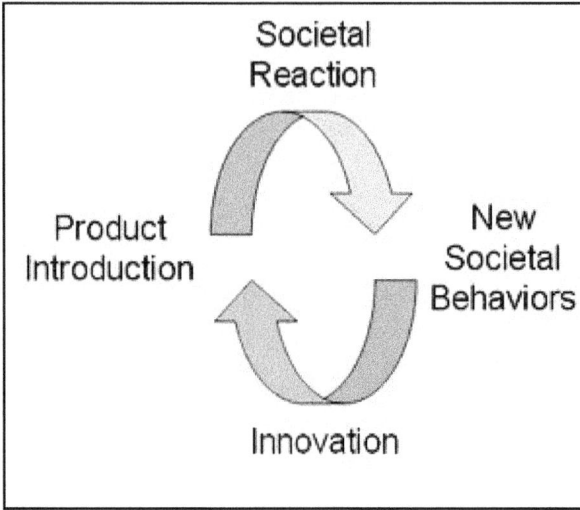

*"You fight with momentum.
There are only a few types of surprises and direct actions."*

Sun Tzu's The Art of War 5:2:20-21

"Demoralize the enemy from within by surprise, terror, sabotage, assassination. This is the war of the future."

Adolf Hitler

General Principle: Momentum amid chaos creates a psychological competitive advantage.

Situation:

In the generally chaotic conditions of competition, no one's actions truly control the situation. The situation as a whole is determined by the complex, unpredictable interactions of actions and events in the environment (3.2.1 Environmental Dominance). However, when we perceive that someone has momentum within a chaotic situation, that perception alone creates a psychological advantage. For those who understand its nature, that short-term subjective advantage can be transformed into longer-term, objective gains in position.

Opportunity:

A psychological divide separates those who have used a surprise from those who were taken by surprise. Those who use surprise are seen on both sides of this divide as 1) understanding and controlling the situation, 2) being prepared for the surprising event, and potentially having other surprises in addition to the followup. This situation increases the uncertainty and fear for those who have been surprised. Their worry about what may happen next, diffusing their focus and increasing the chances that they will leave an opening (3.1.4 Openings). Meanwhile, those who used surprise focus on its results looking for an opening to exploit (1.7.2 Goal Focus). This focus is the difference between having and lacking momentum.

Key Methods:

The following key methods describe how we leverage the psychological nature of surprise to create momentum.

1. The gap between having and lacking momentum is subjective. This subjective difference can be easily transformed into objective differences in position. This depends on our ability to create the proper mental states in others and take advantage of them (1.3.1 Competitive Comparison).

2. Those who have been surprised must leave an opening for us. As always, our actions to create surprise do not create momentum. Those actions must work through others, who create the opening for us. If the opening is left, as it usually is, we can make huge gains, However, as always, this is a matter of probability not certainty. If our opponents are not truly surprised, they may still adjust in time to stop us (3.2 Opportunity Creation).

3. We must immediately move to exploit the opening created by the surprise of others. Our response must assume that an opening will be created. By starting on our followup *before* the opening is there, we set the stage for building momentum. Our hope is that our speed will not give others the time to recover (5.3 Reaction Time).

4. Our move must consume our opponent's psychological resources rather than our physical ones. It cannot endanger our existing position by using resources vital for our defense. Instead, it should be designed to exhaust our opponents psychological resources as they try to understand the situation. If an opening is not left, we lose little. If one is left, we keep up the competitive psychological pressure on opponents (5.4 Minimizing Action).

5. The move must objectively improve our competitive position. We change subjective perceptions because it is less costly than changing objective positions, but that work is wasted unless our actions transform that subjective advantage into objective ones. Momentum is confirmed when people can confirm those objective gains (3.6 Leveraging Subjectivity).

Illustration:

Let us illustrate these ideas with an illustration from American football.

1. The gap between having and lacking momentum is subjective. During a sports contest, a play can result in a surprising turn of the tide such as an interception in football.

2. Those who have been surprised must leave an opening for us. The sudden change of offense and defense puts the intercepted team at an immediate disadvantage, emotionally unprepared for the next play.

3. We must immediately move to exploit the opening created by the surprise of others. The offense often takes advantage of this weakness by attempting a big play, for example, a long touchdown pass.

4. Our move must consume our opponent's psychological resources rather than our physical ones. This play works much more often than it would under normal circumstances. This is not because the defending team is physically less capable but because it is still recovering psychologically from the surprise.

5. The move must objectively improve our competitive position. If the turnover results in a score, the change in momentum is confirmed. If no score results from the surprise, the momentum of the intercepting team is neutralized.

7.1.3 Standards and Innovation

Sun Tzu's seven key methods on the methodology of creativity.

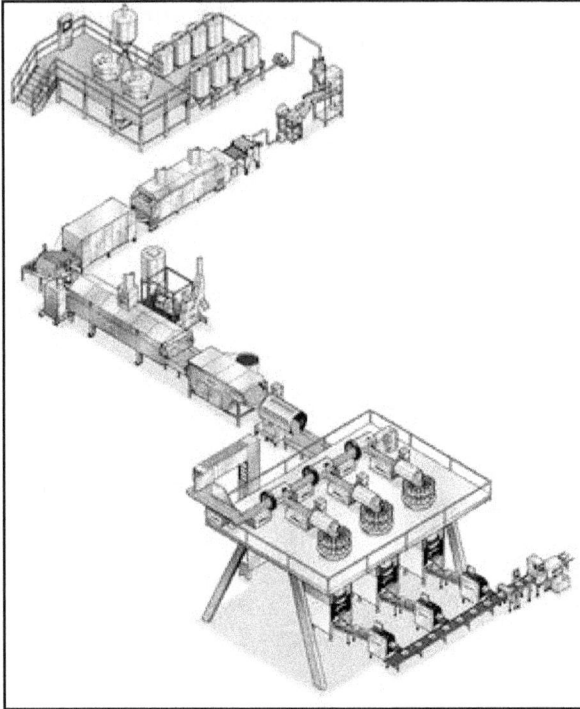

"It is the same in all battles.
You use a direct approach to engage the enemy.
You use surprise to win."

Sun Tzu's The Art of War 5:2:1-3

"Innovation distinguishes between a leader and a
follower."

Steve Jobs

General Principle: The best balance of standards and innovation in competition is the opposite of the best balance in production.

Situation:

We live in an age of linear thinking where we are taught to rely on systematic pre-planned steps to address problems. Within the controlled environments of our schools, we are taught to obey instructions. Workers on the production line repeat standard steps. In production environments, innovation occurs relatively rarely. It usually comes from decisions outside those doing the work. Constant creativity by the workers on the line would disrupt the process of standard production. The problem is that this balance of standards and innovation is completely different in competitive environments.

Opportunity:

In competition, innovation is never external to the strategic process. It is an inherent part of it. Our opportunity is that most people do not realize this, at least at first. Standards are the basis of our creativity. Our creativity is the basis for developing our new standards (3.2.3 Complementary Opposites). Creativity can never disrupt competition. It always enhances it. Without the use of both standards and creativity, direct action and surprise, we can never create the strategic momentum necessary to win success. While production favors standards over innovation, competition favors innovation over standards. Both are still required, but in the competitive environment, everyone is a decision-maker, responsible for improving the process.

Key Methods:

The following key methods describe the roles of standards and innovation in competition.

1. Competitive creativity is necessary because every competitive situation is more unique than the same. We learn standard competitive methods to address the many aspects of competitive situations that repeat themselves, but each of these standard approaches also requires creativity. Creativity addresses the unique content in every situation (7.3 Strategic Innovation).

2. *Strategic standards require instantly responding appropriately to conditions*. Standards give us speed because we don't have time to craft every response from scratch. Our basic responses must be automatic, learned from drill and practice. The faster we recognize situations and respond, the more often we will be successful (6.0 Situation Response).

3. *Our use of creativity and surprise must be reflexive as well.* We must automatically implement all of our generic responses to conditions in a creative way. Creativity in using standard responses can also be practiced (6.1.1 Conditioned Reflexes).

4. *Situations contain multiple conditions whose responses must be creatively combined*. Situations are unique because they combined different sets of conditions in different ways. The combination of responses required is itself a unique prescription for the situation (6.2.1 Campaign Flow).

5. *As others learn our patterns of response, we must creatively adjust our responses to their evolving reactions*. We act in competition in order to get a set of desired responses. The standard responses work because they get the responses we desire. When we understand why they work, we can keep one step ahead of everyone by adapting those methods to their learning curve (2.3.1 Action and Reaction).

6. *We must creatively adapt to the continual changes of climate and position*. Shifts in climate change our position automatically. Our ability to spot the opportunities and new resources from our competitive arena (1.3.1 Competitive Comparison).

7. *The more creative our responses, the more productive our competitive moves will be*. The more creative we are, the more we are perceived as having momentum. Others will find it difficult to predict our moves making it difficult for people to hinder our progress. Being seen as unpredictable is always a competitive advantage (2.3.2 Reaction Unpredictability).

Illustration:

Let us illustrate these ideas with an illustration from a sales presentation.

1. Competitive creativity is necessary because every competitive situation is more unique than the same. A salesperson that simply repeats the same sales pitch to every client is not going to be successful.

2. Strategic standards require instantly responding appropriately to conditions. A salesperson must know how to instantly respond with the best proven answers to the common objections that he or she hears from customers.

3. Our use of creativity and surprise must be reflexive as well. The most successful salespeople automatically use the unique perspectives and situations of clients in their sales presentations.

4. Situations contain multiple conditions whose responses must be creatively combined. Great salespeople are like medical diagnosticians, able to separate different symptoms into a prescription that makes the best possible sense.

5. As others learn our patterns of response, we must creatively adjust our responses to their evolving reactions. A salesperson realizes that the more established the customer, the more something new and different is required to interest and hold them.

6. We must creatively adapt to the continual changes of climate and position. Great salespeople always start with what is changing as the basis for their sales presentation because they realize that it is change that both worries us and captures our imagination.

7. The more creative our responses, the more productive our competitive moves will be. A great salesperson is like an entertainer. The customer never knows what to expect but is always stimulated by the result.

7.2.0 Standards First

Sun Tzu's seven key methods on the role of standards in creating connections with others.

"You win a war by first assuring yourself of victory. Only afterward do you look for a fight."
Sun Tzu's The Art of War 4:3:24-25

"First impressions are often the truest, as we find (not infrequently) to our cost, when we have been wheedled out of them by plausible professions or studied actions."
William Hazlitt

General Principle: We must use the standard, proven methods to initiate a competitive move.

Situation:

All moves have a beginning. At the beginning of a move, we have the least information about the situation into which we are getting involved (2.1.1 Information Limits]). When our move brings us in contact with new people, we know little about them and how they will react. Among potential supporters, a bad initial impression is costly to overcome. Since these people know little about us and our intentions, they are likely to be suspicious since everyone's first reaction should be to defend.

Opportunity:

When we make initial contact with others, we have an opportunity to control their first impressions. We have the opportunity to create a good impression. That impression provides a leverage point, creating expectations that we can use to advance our position. Our initial actions have a disproportionate effect, a leveraging effect, on how people react to us and how we are likely to proceed. Initial contact is a natural leverage point, if we know how to use it.

Key Methods:

The following key methods determine how we should act in making our initial contacts with people.

1. Standards are the foundation of all contact and connection. This is true whether we are talking about connections among people or among communication systems. Without shared standard, no communication is possible. This communication starts with a common language, which provides the lowest common denominator of connection, but it includes layer after layer of cultural context that ties people together, including standard of courtesy and professionalism (7.2.1 Proven Methods).

2. We must initiate all contacts by invoking standards. In practical terms, these standards are both social and professional. In the world of technology, we call the initiation of communication between systems a "handshake." The same ideas applies to personal communication. If we start by being so different that others simply don't know what to expect from us, we will have a difficult time making any connections. If we want to connect with others, we get started on the right foot by doing what is expected. Objectively, we use standard methods because they are proven to work. Subjectively, we use standards because human psychology requires a standard reference point around which to form an impression (1.2 Subobjective Positions).

3. *When we first connect with others, we must minimize chaos*. The initiation of contact is chaotic and novel enough. In today's networked world, new contacts are often interruptions in the expected order of events. Chaos creates work and stress for us, wasting time, effort, and resources. We increase our chances of connecting by minimizing the work required. While we no longer require a formal introduction to meet new people, we can expect better responses if we use every social and professional standard (2.3.1 Action and Reaction).

4. *This question of standards quickly becomes a question of shared values*. After the initial handshake, people quickly move to questions about goals and motivation. We build on a shared acceptance of our mutual self-interest. While we don't have to share all our values, we have to share our respect for our different resources and that our differences for the basis for a mutually rewarding exchange (1.6 Mission Values).

5. *We generate strong initial impressions by using existing expectations*. We form our first impressions with a minimum of information. First contact is a leverage point where a little information goes a long way. We must play an expected role to generate the type of impression that we desire. We attempt to duplicate a typical experience that is easier for others to categorize. This first impression then becomes a commonly understood point for the rest of the relationship (1.1 Position Paths)

6. *We can shape future expectations more easily starting with a clear first impression*. Sun Tzu's strategy requires controlling other people's expectations. If we don't know people's first impressions, we have a much more difficult time shaping their future

opinions. We surprise people by exceeding their expectation. For this method to work, people must think they know what to expect. People simply cannot relate to concepts that are too new and different (7.2.2 Preparing Expectations).

7. *Sun Tzu's mental models give us a simple set of standard starting points for competitive situations*. Sun Tzu's strategy is based on the archetypal concepts of comparing positions and relationship. Despite its depth of detail and specialized language, it maps to a basic model of the world that most people already carry in their minds. It is easy to explain Sun Tzu's concepts using analogies in so many different competitive areas because people start with many of its preconceptions without knowing it (2.2.2 Mental Models).

Illustration:

Let us illustrate these ideas discussing the importance of user interface in introducing new technologies.

1. *Standards are the foundation of all contact and connection*. New technologies must be build on existing understanding. For example, personal computers sold only to a small technical segment of the population until software such as word-processing and electronic spreadsheet created an easy starting point for regular people to connect with computers.

2. *We must initiate all contacts by invoking standards*. Hundreds of calculating programs for computers came and went before the first "electronic spreadsheet" like today's Excel was introduced. Modeled directly on the existing accounting spreadsheets, it gave people an easy entry point into using computing to address problems.

3. *When we first connect with others, we must minimize chaos*. When computer operating systems required users to master a new language, responding with cryptic error messages, people quickly rejected the experience. As user interfaces became more graphic, they allowed users to understand the computer environment by connecting them to more physical environments.

4. *This question of standards quickly becomes a question of shared values*. A given user interface design results from a set of values, often unconsciously expressed. The original cryptic computer interfaces placed their value on arcane knowledge of users. That knowledge created a private, exclusive club. The modern, graphical designs put a premium on simplicity and clarity.

5. *We generate strong initial impressions by using existing expectations*. When we encounter a new device, we rely on our knowledge of similar devices to figure out how to use it. We use visual and other cues to understand the underlying template used for design. When the controls and words used are unfamiliar, making it hard to know what to do, we form a negative first impression that is very difficult to overcome. When they are familiar working in ways we already understand, we get a positive first impression.

6. *We can shape future expectations more easily starting with a clear first impression*. Devices can lead us to new capabilities more easily when they start from familiar starting points. Leading software companies all realize this by designing their family of products around familiar formats. No matter what desktop browser you are using now, it probably has a menu that starts "File Edit View" following the original design of Microsoft applications.

7. *Sun Tzu's mental models give us a simple set of standard starting points for competitive situations*. User interface design falls within the realm of production and control rather than competition and strategy, but the market for under interface design is competitive. Designs for interfaces must minimize barriers to usability (4.5.2 Surface Barriers) and create easy situations for users (6.4.2 Easy Situations) are always going to be more popular than those that don't.

7.2.1 Proven Methods

Sun Tzu's eight key methods for identifying and recognizing the limits of best practices.

Effective Competition		
	Winners	**Losers**
Efficient Production — Valuable	**Best Practices**	No Difference
Efficient Production — Costly	No Difference	**Worst Practices**

"Influence events.
Think about opportunities in terms of methods you can
control."

Sun Tzu's The Art of War 1:3:4-5

"It's all very well in practice, but it will never work in
theory."

French Proverb

General Principle: A given set of proven methods combine a formula for production with a formula for competition.

Situation:

Leveraging the forces of our environment without know-how is impossible. Our world works because it is built on thousands of years of accumulated human knowledge. It requires work to prove which techniques, methods processes, and activities work best to accomplish a certain set of goals. As our technical knowledge has grown more complex, we each master a smaller and smaller piece of the whole. As our success at manipulating our environment has grown, more and more of us are isolated from the hard realities of nature. Complexity leads to chaos if the connections tying together our know-how are not preserved and passed down from generation to generation.

Opportunity:

Sun Tzu's system of innovation is based upon knowing how the world works, both in production and in competition. The value of competition is that it naturally separates what works from what works better. If we focus on what has been proven to work, progress using innovation is much easier. When we must base our creativity on the thousands of years of strategic learning, it becomes fairly easy to do.

Key Methods:

The following eight key methods describe what we must understand in order to use proven methods as a basis for innovation.

1. Proven methods represent techniques, processes, and activities that are more effective at delivering a desired outcome than alternatives methods. This rule means that there is an objective reality whose natural laws are best leveraged with some actions over others. While our knowledge of these laws is always limited, the effectiveness of a given set of actions is not merely a matter of belief or perspective but based on an underlying reality (1.2 Subobjective Positions).

2. Best methods are proven by comparing the results of alternative approaches. We cannot determine best practices merely by our intellectual analysis, which is always based solely on our limited knowledge. Superior methods can only be determined in the arena of competition where they outperform less effective methods (1.3.1 Competitive Comparison).

3. Best practices represent a snapshot of our limited knowledge not complete knowledge about what is possible. Over time, better practices are discovered through the competition of ideas. Most new approaches are proven not to work, but eventually better methods are discovered (1.2.2 Exploiting Exploration).

4. Proven methods combine a set of competitive methods with a set of production methods. What is proven in any given case is the combination. The comparative advantage of any given combination can lie at either side of this equation or emerge from the combination of both. As complementary opposites, these two separate realms of skills are two sides of the same coin (1.9 Competition and Production).

5. Small advances to proven methods are more likely to be successful than big ones. This rule is the basis for successful innovation. If we start with a large base of knowledge about strategy, we need to add only a small drop of creativity. Strategically, the best innovations are those that leverage the most existing knowledge. (5.5 Focused Power)

6. Any attempt to innovate too many aspects of a best practice is extremely likely to fail. A working process works like the links in a chain. It works because each link supports the others. Any attempt at innovation that replaces too many links in that chain depends upon too many unproven links. While large innovation can rarely succeed, their rate of success conforms to the power law distribution, which calls for a great many small advances for every large one (1.8.4 Probabilistic Process).

7. Proven production methods require less innovation than competitive methods. Models of production are relatively easy to understand because they exist in areas where we have greater knowledge and control. Production methods are based on duplication so they are by their very nature, more easily duplicated (1.9.2 Span of Control).

8. Proven competitive methods require an innovation to deal with unique conditions. Unlike production environments where conditions are controlled, competition exists in an environment that is beyond our control. While some general aspects of competitive methods can be proven to work in similar conditions, the unique and shifting nature of competitive environments require constant adaptation (1.9.1 Production Comparisons).

Illustration:

Let us illustrate these key methods by discussing the introduction of a successful new electronic product.

1. Proven methods represent techniques, processes, and activities that are more effective at delivering a desired outcome than alternatives methods. No matter how revolutionary it seems, a product must be built with familiar controls. Inside, it consists primarily of proven components.

2. Best methods are only proven by comparing the results of alternative approaches. Think about everything that goes into making that device work. All have been chose because someone thought they would work best, but only the success of the product on the market proves those decisions correct.

3. Best practices represent a snapshot of our limited knowledge not complete knowledge about what is possible. Each generation of products represents an advance over previous ones. No generation of products is so perfect that it cannot be improved over time.

4. Proven methods combine a set of competitive methods with a set of production methods. The product is assembled in factories using standard methods. It is marketed in existing media based on existing brand images in ways previous products have proven. It is distributed by existing product channels. 99.9% of what makes a product successful both in production and competition is standard, proven technology.

5. Small advances to proven methods are more likely to be successful than big ones. What makes the product "new" is perhaps 1% of innovation added to make it different from previous generations of product.

6. *Any attempt to innovate too many aspects of a best practice is extremely likely to fail.* For that "new" product to work, it must have a lot of old in it. Products that involve too much innovation fail either in production, because they cannot be made efficiently, or in competition, because they cannot be effectively understood by their potential customers.

7. *Proven production methods require less innovation than competitive methods.* Almost all new successful electronic products require very little less innovation in their production methods.

8. *Proven competitive methods require an innovation to deal with unique conditions*. Almost all new successful electronic products require an innovative take on the customer needs that they must address.

7.2.2 Preparing Expectations

Sun Tzu's eight key methods on how we shape other people's expectation.

"*Chaos gives birth to control.*
Fear gives birth to courage.
Weakness gives birth to strength."
Sun Tzu's The Art of War 1:3:4-5

"*The quality of expectations determines the quality of*
our action."

A. Godin

General Principle: We shape people's expectations by leveraging the certainty of hope against the confusion of fear.

Situation:

When we participate in a controlled process, our expectations are nothing more than assuming everyone else involved will do their job. In the chaotic arena of competition, the term "expectation" takes on a different meaning. We have no overall specification of anyone's responsibilities before we come to an agreement with them. Everyone's decisions regarding their commitments depend upon their own individual goals and the conditions that affect them over time. What do we expect them to do? Only to behave in accordance with their own best interests as they see those interests.

Opportunity:

Since people long for predictability, our opportunity is in controlling their expectations, that is, giving them what they long for. In chaotic competitive environments, we want to know what to expect from others. We realize that we can only learn what to expect from our interactions with them. We gravitate toward those whose interests we can understand. We prefer those who promote their interests in a consistent and dependable way. Though individual actions cannot be predicted, we develop expectations developed upon our experience. These expectations take the form of probabilities (1.8.4 Probabilistic Process).

Key Methods:

The process of setting expectations is a feedback loop that depends on eight key methods.

1. Controlling people's expectations is valuable whether or not we expect to confirm them. Sometimes, we control people's expectations so that we can confirm their beliefs. Other times, we control expectations to set people up for a surprise. We can use either approach to win supporters or frustrate opponents depending on the situation (2.3.1 Action and Reaction).

2. People want events or results in an external, competitive environment to be as predictable as those in controlled internal environments. This desire is a result of our education for working in a linear, controlled environments. The truth is that the our expectations in a controlled environment are inherently more reliable than expectations in competitive environments. The fact that people don't understand the key differences in these two environments gives us our strategic leverage point since our expectations for the future are likely to be much more open than those of others (1.9 Competition and Production).

3. To control people's expectations, we must leverage their natural balance between optimism and pessimism. People form their expectations to minimize their confusion while maximizing their happiness. We want to believe the future is predictable, but we hedge our bets because at a gut level we know it is not. A too pessimistic view of the future is depressing, but a too optimistic view is risky and often leads to frustration. Both states of mind undermine our happiness. These opposing states of mind are complementary opposites. The balance between them shifts back and forth depending on character and conditions. To create people's expectations, we must leverage this balance, working to bring the extreme back in balance. (3.2.3 Complementary Opposites).

4. All our words and actions signal our intentions to form others expectations of us. Actions are more costly than words so they are more believable, but we don't have to understand all the details of signaling theory to understand that everything we do tells others about us. Our dress, our manners, what we talk about, and how we talk all give people signals regarding our character and intentions. We can offer honest signals or dishonest ones. We can also offer intentionally confusing signals. People can choose to believe or disbelieve our signals whether those signals are honest or not (2.1.3 Strategic Deception).

5. We shape the expectations of others by offering them a predictive model that conforms with their judgments. Past judgments are the only basis for future expectations. We play into the confirmation bias, people's tendency to search for or interpret information to conform with their viewpoints. One of the advantages of mastering Sun Tzu's principles is that it provides a big, picture model of how the world works that conforms with what people learn from their own experience but never learn to express. We shape their expectations based upon demonstrating that we share ***their***

understanding of what is important in a situation by offering a more complete picture of that situations (2.5 The Big Picture).

6. People's pessimism arises from their confusion about competitive chaos. Just as people's plans collide in competitive environments, our expectations also collide. Our expectations can collide with the expectations of others and with our own conflicting expectations. The result is both frustration and confusion, which we seek to avoid by gravitating toward points of view that protect us from frustration but actually do not offer more certainty (7.1 Order from Chaos).

7. People's optimism arises from their desires and their goals. Whether it is realistic or not, we all want others to act the way we want them to. All our expectations are ultimately about our goals and desires. While our expectations can be either optimistic or pessimistic, both directions concern our desire for gain and fear of less. We cannot leverage people's expectations unless our initial contacts with them help us understand those goals and desires (1.6 Mission Values).

8. We improve our certainty in the expectation of others by seeking feedback. We ideally look for confirmation in people's deeds, but words can be useful as well. We want this feedback whether it confirms our success in shaping expectations or not. When our feedback confirms a set of expectations, we are in a much better position to know how to act to satisfy our goals (2.3.3 Likely Reactions).

Illustration:

Let us illustrate these principles by discussing how betting controls the expectations of others in a poker game.

1. Controlling people's expectations is valuable whether or not we expect to confirm them. In poker, everyone is an opponent. We use our betting to establish patterns of behavior that our opponents think they can use to predict our actions in a given situation.

2. People want events or results in an external, competitive environment to be as predictable as those in controlled internal environments. Amateurs understand the role of bluffing and the mathematics well enough to think that people are more predictable than they are. Professionals use these expectations against them, using false tells to set them up for future disappointment.

3. To control people's expectations, we must leverage their natural balance between optimism and pessimism. In a poker game, everyone is shifting back and forth between their greed and fear. We use their greed to encourage them to bet a losing hand. We use their fear to bluff them out of winning hands.

4. All our words and actions signal our intentions to form others expectations of us. In the case of poker, we bet or raise to signal a strong hand. We check or call or fold to signal a weak one. We also have a variety of other behaviors that also provide signals, but those behaviors, like words, are cheap. It is the betting that sends the strongest signals and we establish our patterns of behavior though the course of a game.

5. We shape the expectations of others by offering them a predictive model that conforms with their judgments. Our opponents develop their expectations about us, whether we are a tight player or loose, aggressive or conservative, depending on our signals.

6. People's pessimism arises from their confusion about competitive chaos. When our betting follows no meaningful pattern or violates the patterns that we have established in the past, people are confused about what we hold. In those situations, they are more likely to be cautious.

7. People's optimism arises from their desires and their goals. When our betting follows a certain pattern and others think they know whether or not our hand is strong or weak, people grow more optimistic about making the right decisions.

8. We improve our certainty in the expectation of others by seeking feedback. When we seek to encourage their betting and they bet, we confirm our model of their expectations. When we seek to discourage their betting and they do not bet, we also confirm our understanding of how we have shaped their expectations.

7.3.0 Strategic Innovation

Sun Tzu's six key methods defining a simple system for innovation.

"There are only a few basic colors.
Yet you can always mix them.
You can never see all the shades of victory."
Sun Tzu's The Art of War 5:2:14-16

"Innovation is not the product of logical thought,
although the result is tied to logical structure."
Albert Einstein

General Principle: Systematic strategic innovation comes from working on the smallest possible parts of a process.

Situation:

The creativity of surprise is vital to every aspect of good competitive strategy, but most of us do not understand what strategic innovation is and how we accomplish it. We are taught two ideas about invention that work against the everyday creativity that we need in strategy.

- First, we think innovation is a flash of inspiration, a "great idea" that just pops into our mind.
- Next, we think that these great ideas are the realm of special geniuses who are far out of the mainstream of regular thought.

This view of creativity is useless for the purpose of strategy. First, we cannot wait for ideas to pop into our heads because we need ideas every day. Second, strategy requires small dashes of creativity based on a firm foundation of practical knowledge. We all have a million ideas, and very few of them are great, but that doesn't matter. More to the point, they are irrelevant to the need at hand. If anything, great ideas are a distraction because, though they seem great when we have them. Very, very few prove to be valuable at all to the situation at hand.

Opportunity:

People think inventiveness is difficult, depending on an inborn ability. In school, we are taught to think of inventors as rare, exotic creatures. The truth is that strategic innovation is easy and almost automatic once we master its perspective. Few recognize this possibility.

In a world in which people are trained simply to follow instructions, most of us simply overlook creative approaches that are right in front of us. Strategically, innovation is not a matter of creating something that is completely new. New ideas have a low-probability of success. If we want a high-probability of success, our creativity must be based on what has been proven to work in the past (7.2 Standards First). Our opportunity is in mastering a method that allows us to create something new whenever we have the need.

Key Methods:

Sun Tzu's mental model for understanding how to successfully innovate in a consistent way requires mastering six simple methods.

1. Strategic innovation requires decisions about parts rather than wholes. Up to this point, we have been making competitive decisions based on the situation as a whole. Innovation and surprise focus our decisions on the smallest possible pieces of the whole. Situation awareness is a matter of putting together a big picture from little pieces of information. Strategic creativity reverses that process, breaking things down into smaller pieces to identify specific targets for innovation. (3.2.4 Emptiness and Fullness).

2. Proven methods must be broken into their component parts. This process starts by breaking down things into their separate components. Everything developed by the human mind is made up of smaller components. Machines are made of parts. Processes are a series of steps. Recipes are a number of ingredients. Sun Tzu's strategy offers a systematic method for identifying these parts. This process of breaking components down can go on indefinitely, since each component can itself be broken down into finer components (7.3.1 Expected Elements).

3. Everyday innovation simply rearranges existing parts. This is the most common and easiest form of innovation. When we have a comprehensive process for breaking anything into its components, that same system tells us how they can be arranged. It requires no new ingredients or components. The existing order of steps or components creates a certain set of expectations. Any change in order creates an innovation that upset expectations and creates surprise. We examine how these components work together and ask ourselves if they will still work if we simply rearrange them to create something unexpected (7.3.2 Elemental Rearrangement).

4. Deeper innovation requires eliminating an existing part and possibly replacing it with a new one. This is the less common and more challenging form of innovation. It requires a process to work differently, without an existing component or with a replacement component. One advantage of this approach is that the existing order of steps or components can be otherwise maintained. We examine how these components work together and ask ourselves if they will still work if we simply eliminate a part or replace it (7.3.3 Creative Innovation).

5. The change to proven methods should be made in as small an increment as possible. This approach minimizes mistakes and reduces potential wasted efforts (5.4 Minimizing Action).

6. Innovations that are too small to create surprise must be combined for impact. One of the principles for creating surprise is that the change must be large enough to force attention. When we improve in small increments, individual changes lack the impact needed to get attention. In these situations, small changes can be made in secret and unveiled together to generate the desired result (7.1.1 Creating Surprise).

Illustration:

Let us illustrate how these key methods are used in business by examining the success of Starbucks in changing the model for selling cups of coffee.

1. Strategic innovation requires decisions about parts rather than wholes. In the end, we still go into a retail store and get a cup of coffee with milk just like we did before Starbucks. What Starbucks changed was parts of the process.

2. Proven methods must be broken into their component parts. In the original process, beans were ground ahead of time. Coffee was brewed ahead of time. A customer then ordered a cup of coffee. The brewed coffee was poured. Then the customer added their own milk or cream. The coffee shop environment provided was cold and sparse.

3. Everyday innovation simply rearranges existing parts. Starbucks used the same key components were the same, but the order was changed. The order is taken. The coffee is then ground fresh. The coffee is then brewed instantly. The milk is added warm so as not to cool the coffee. Then the drink is served. The environment was warm, inviting people to linger.

4. Deeper innovation requires eliminating an existing part and possibly replacing it with a new one. Starbucks replaced drip brewing with the steam brewing used in Europe, which required a darker roast of bean.

5. The change to proven methods should be made in as small an increment as possible. Nothing here was revolutionary. All of these methods had long been used and proven in Europe.

6. Innovations that are too small to create surprise must be combined for impact. Many of the changes Startbucks instituted appeared before, but in isolation, they were not enough to make an impression.

7.3.1 Expected Elements

Sun Tzu's seven key methods on dividing processes and systems into components.

"There are only a few notes in the scale.
Yet you can always rearrange them.
You can never hear every song of victory."
Sun Tzu's The Art of War 5:2:11-13

"Both traditions want people to think. They want people
who are problem solvers and can take apart a problem
and put it back together again."
Marlene Barron

General Principle: Creativity starts by separating components in terms of space, time, formula, and purpose.

Situation:

Linear thinking [2] requires using pre-planned processes, working with systems and machines. We are trained to use these systems without understanding them. We can start to think that we need not and cannot understand how systems work, but even things that can be hard to make can be easy to understand. We are not taught a comprehensive method for taking existing things apart to see how they are made to work. We take the existing components for granted. When we use products, machines, and processes, we are not aware of the parts. The human mind filters out what is expected and taken for granted.

Opportunity:

Sun Tzu teaches that opportunities are hidden (3.2.2 Opportunity Invisibility [3]). As we lose sight of the components of which things are made, an opening is created. We want to identify overlooked components that we can exploit. Those who take the time to break things into their parts can use this understanding to their strategic advantage.

Key Methods:

The following seven key methods describe Sun Tzu's systematic process for identifying the elements that can be rearranged or replaced to create surprise.

1. Everything that people put together can be taken apart. Unlike the complexity that arises in complex, adaptive systems, which is beyond our understanding, human constructions can be broken down into smaller pieces. Machines are made of parts. Processes are a series of steps. Recipes consist of ingredients. When any of these are taken apart, we better understood it. Every created object and every intentional action is made of small components (7.2.1 Proven Methods [4]).

2. Steps in a process are events arranged in time. Arrangements in time describe steps in a process, each having a length of time, a place in the sequence, and a frequency of repetition (1.8.3 Cycle Time [5]).

3. Parts are arranged in a physical relationship to each other to create organization in space. Arrangements in space describes how parts are put together in a machine or a picture, having shape, relative size, and attributes of interaction (4.4 Strategic Distance [6]).

4. The relative portions of ingredients in a recipe are the qualitative parts of the formula. Portions in a formula are based on relative, measurable quantities. Formulas describe how ingredients are put together where those ingredients have different characteristics and interact with each other. The relative quantity of each of those components is the key to the recipe (2.2.2 Mental Models [7]).

5. Every step, part, or ingredient in a system fills a specific need, and all needs are potential openings. Systems, relationships, and processes satisfy people's needs. Whether people recognize it or not, each part, each step, each ingredient satisfies a piece of that need, filling a small opening. To understand the component, we must understand its value, meaning, and purpose as part of the whole (2.4.5 Mission Perspective [8]).

6. Every step, part, or ingredient of a system creates a specific expectation. Just as we take the expected for granted, our brains are geared to recognize the abnormal, the things that are out of place. By shifting from what is normal, we have the opportunity to get people's attention and create surprise (7.2.2 Preparing Expectations [9]).

7. Rearranging parts may or may not improve efficiency, but it always creates surprise. When we focus on internal production, efficiency is most important, but when we focus on external competition, the surprise is most important. From the surprise, we seize initiative, creating momentum. To create surprise, we don't have to improve the process. All we have to do is violate expectations (1.9 Competition and Production [10]).

Illustration:

Sun Tzu describes this method for understanding in terms of sound, sight, and flavor. Let us combine his description with a description of the system, the computer, that I am using to write this.

1. Everything that people put together can be taken apart. We can take apart computers. We can see how their pieces fit together. Those who are in the computer business must take them apart in order to improve them.

2. Steps in a process are events arranged in time. Using a computer is a process. Activities follow in a certain sequence, requiring a certain amount of time. I must turn it on, select a program to run, choose what documents I want to work on, start working, save my work, and so on.

3. Parts are arranged in a physical relationship to each other to create organization in space. As a machine, it has physical components organized in space. I expect the keyboard to be below the screen, the keys to be arranged on it in a certain way, the touch pad to be in front of the keyboard, and the touch pad buttons in front of it.

4. The relative portions of ingredients in a recipe are the qualitative parts of the formula. In a computer, the quantitative elements are the size of its memory, its screen, its disk-drive and so on. Software depends on certain minimum quantities in order to function.

5. Every step, part, or ingredient in a system fills a specific need, and all needs are potential openings. We need a keyboard to get data into the system. That need can be fulfilled by other forms of data entry than typing. We need a screen for data output. Other forms of data output can satisfy that need.

6. Every step, part, or ingredient of a system creates a specific expectation. I have certain expectations for how the software will work because I know the steps that have worked in the past to perform a certain function. The same is true of the physical parts, such as the layout of the keyboard. For certain computer parts--the power button, the volume control, etc. I have no expectation because there is no standard design or location, so those components have no affect on expectations.

7. Rearranging parts may or may not improve efficiency, but it always creates surprise. To create surprise, we must change the order of events or elements. We initially meet expectations by satisfying those expectations, but we surprise by violating them, arranging the component in a novel way. For example in process, computers increasingly skip the "select program" part, loading the appropriate program instantly when we pick the document we want to work on. Small Web-book laptops assume we are going to access the internet and load a browser. In hardware, tablet computers use touch screens as virtual keyboards. This opens the possibility of creating a virtual keyboard that could display programmable keys that display their user-defined functions.

7.3.2 Elemental Rearrangement

Sun Tzu's six key methods for seeing invention as rearranging proven elements.

"There are only a few flavors.
Yet you can always blend them.
You can never taste all the flavors of victory."
Sun Tzu's The Art of War 5:2:17-19

"We must always change, renew, rejuvenate ourselves;
otherwise we harden."
Johann Wolfgang von Goethe

General Principle: Surprise comes from rearranging components in terms of time, space, and formula.

Situation:

Constructive strategy requires innovating in a minimum of time. To this, we must quickly identify the separate components that shape the situation (7.3.1 Expected Elements). Only then can we see how those elements create certain expectation. However, this knowledge alone doesn't tell us how we can change those elements creatively.

In most of our education, we are trained to use systems, not create new systems. When we use standard systems, we operate within a controlled area (7.2 Standards First). We are comfortable with standards because we know what to expect. However, when we simply operate under standards, we are literally controlled by the system. We are controlled by those who developed those systems for their own \purposes, even though we use those systems for our own benefit.

Opportunity:

If we want to get more control over our lives, we must develop systems that we control. Whenever we operate in any competitive arena, we work outside of the limits of existing control. We have the opportunity to create new areas of control, but we can only do this by creating our own systems, procedures, and formulas. Controlling our own behavior is a good start, but real power comes from understanding the effect of our systems on others (2.3.1 Action and Reaction).

Developing new methods from scratch is both risky and difficult (7.2.1 Proven Methods). Existing systems influence our expectations by making us think that we cannot step outside of them (7.2.2 Preparing Expectations). We are taught to treat existing processes as sacred. They are not sacred. They are simply productive. In competition, the value of innovating systems is that they create surprise and change momentum.

Key Methods:

The following key methods explain the process for reordering elements for strategic advantage.

1. All changes to existing systems that violate expectations are strategically useful. The primary goal of strategy is to surprise. While changes that make systems more productive are useful, we start with a much simpler goal of creating what interrupts the normal flow of events (5.4 Minimizing Action).

2. We must identify the components parts in the situation by dividing it in time, space, and formula. Time components arrange tasks in a certain sequence. Space components are arranged in physical and psychological space. Formula components have different proportions creating a formula. At this level of innovation, we are not changing the components. We are using the existing proven methods. Because the end result is made of all the parts of the original system, the new version will "work," at least in some sense of the word. It will, however, work differently (7.2 Standards First).

3. We must identify the expectations these components create. We normally see components in terms of their function. Each part of a system or each step in a process does something specific. We must take that recognition one step further. That function creates an expectation. We need to see each of these components in terms of the specific expectations that they create (7.2.2 Preparing Expectations).

4. We must consider reshuffling or reordering components in time, space, and formula to confound expectations. These three are a) reordering components in time, performing tasks in a different sequence, b) rearranging components in physical and psychological space, setting up different interactions, c) changing proportions in the formula, adjusting their relative quantities in small ways (7.3.1 Expected Elements).

5. We must pick the quickest and easiest method that inter-rupts expectations. This reshuffling is best if done quickly. Slight changes in order, arrangement, and proportion can dramatically affect the expected situation (7.1.1 Creating Surprise).

6. Some changes will create long-term improvements as well as simple surprises. This happens through trial and error. Because change creates a surprise, every change at the right time is valu-able. However, our strategic need to make constant changes leads naturally to deeper exploration of the system. Eventually we find improved arrangements that are permanent improvements (1.2.2 Exploiting Exploration).

Illustration:

Since innovation happens much more quickly in high-tech, let us use innovation in that arena to demonstrate some of these basic ideas.

1. All changes to existing systems that violate expectations are strategically useful. For example, it is too early to know if the Apple iPad will be a success in terms of innovation, but it is a stra-tegic success because it focuses consumers on the Apple brand and developers on the platform.

2. We must identify the components parts in the situation by dividing it in time, space, and formula. Ordering in time: People pay for a product before using it. Arrangement in space: Computer applications on the mobile device, desktop, or the server. Re-pro-portioning the formula: making an iPod bigger, changing it into a tablet.

3. We must identify the expectations these components create. Ordering in time: People expect to have to decide about the value of a product before buying it. Arrangement in space: People expect to have a mobile device, desktop, or server access before using the applications that run on them. Reproportioning the formula: people expect a certain device size.

4. We must consider reshuffling or reordering components in time, space, and formula to confound expectations. Re-ordering in time: The concept of freeware and free software demonstrations reverses the expectation to pay for a product before using it. Rearrangement in space: Google Apps is a spacial change giving people access to desktop apps from a server environment. Re-proportioning the formula: the iPad changes the expectation of limited screen space in a mobile app.

5. *We must pick the quickest and easiest method that interrupts expectations.* All of these changes were easy for the company making them.

6. *Some changes will create long-term improvements as well as simple surprises.* In the end, all applications may be offered initially as freeware and all may be available on servers. Of course, the iPad tablet's success will create a new direction for future innovation.

7.3.3 Creative Innovation

Sun Tzu's seven key methods on the more advanced methods for innovation.

*"Surprise and direct action give birth to each other.
They are like a circle without end.
You cannot exhaust all their possible combinations!"*
Sun Tzu's The Art of War 5:2:24-26

"If necessity is the mother of invention, discontent is the father of progress."
David Rockefeller

General Principle: Deeper invention requires subtracting, adding, or replacing components.

Situation:

We see the nature of the world as limited. We look at our limited knowledge of our current situation and envision running out of resources. While our regular method of innovation by rearranging elements is quick and easy, we will eventually come up against its limits (7.3.2 Elemental Rearrangement). Since there are limited number of elements in systems, there are also limits on how they can be rearranged. While all arrangements may surprise, only a few rearrangements will be actual improvements. For 2,500 years, the philosophy of limits has been championed by those in power to justify taking more power in an attempt to stop change. In China, the aristocracy suppressed Sun Tzu's philosophy for just this reason.

Opportunity:

Sun Tzu's strategy is diametrically opposed to this point of view of limited resources because those limits are based on our limited knowledge (2.1.1 Information Limits). While our knowledge is always limited, it also grows over time (2.6 Knowledge Leverage). From its beginning 2,500 years ago, Sun Tzu taught that our undiscovered resources were infinite. Time has proven his astounding prediction correct. If we regularly practice using "regular" innovation, we will also eventually discover opportunities for more powerful forms of invention. These methods for creating "special" innovations are never as quick or as certain as simple rearrangement, but they can provide the infinite number of possibilities that our progress demands.

Key Methods:

Sun Tzu offers seven principles of creating innovations with persistent value.

1. Innovation starts as a thought experiment so that we can quickly test the new envisioned system mentally. Unlike rearranging components, more advanced methods of innovation open up many more possibilities. We do not have time to explore them all.

Their result will always have to be tested in the real world. This takes times and resources, which are costly. In using thought experiments, we can work through many possibilities to find the best one very quickly (2.2.2 Mental Models).

2. We must identify the components parts in the situation by dividing it in time, space, and formula. Time components arrange tasks in a certain sequence. Space components are arranged in physical and psychological space. Formula components have different proportions creating a formula. At this level of innovation, we are not changing the components. We are using the existing proven methods. Because the end result is made of all the parts of the original system, the new version will "work," at least in some sense of the word. It will, however, work differently (7.2 Standards First).

3. We attempt to identify components that can be eliminated entirely. We look for ways to eliminate steps in the sequence, the number of components, or the volume of ingredients. This is the easiest method to innovate a process. By definition, simpler systems are better systems. They have fewer costs, are less prone to break, and, when they do break, they are easier to fix. Any innovation that eliminates a component is valuable (4.2 Choosing Non-Action).

4. We attempt to identify components that are proven to work in a similar situation or function. We look for analogous processes, systems, and procedures that have similar steps, components, or ingredients. Seeing analogous parallels gets easier as we are trained in Sun Tzu's system because its strategic system is built on finding parallels in unique situations. The classical Chinese framework of science of the five Chinese classical elements is a system of parallel analogies. We use the key elements in strategic analysis to train the mind to see parallels in situations. Analogous elements can replace each other in innovative arrangements (1.3 Elemental Analysis).

5. We attempt to replace one existing element with an analogous alternative. We look for ways to replace one step in the sequence with a different step. We replace one component or ingredient for a different component or ingredient. Using this method, we try to keep all the other components the same. We are looking for a element that is better in some tangible way or less expensive than the one it replaces (3.1.2 Strategic Profitability).

6. We attempt to add one new element to fill an opening in the existing system. Conceptually, this is very similar to identifying the openings that create opportunities. We use our understanding of similar systems to identify new elements that might work. We look for a place to add one step in the sequence to improve the result. We look for a new component that will make the system better. We look for a new ingredient that will make the formula stronger. Using this method, we try to keep all the other components the same (3.0 Identifying Opportunities).

7. Test the resulting changes to see what the effect is on the whole system. Unlike a rearrangement, that just needs to create surprise, the change here is less likely to work. This means it requires more testing. Until it is tested, we can get no advantage from the surprise it may create because we are as likely to be surprised by the result as our opponents. This final step is critical to the success of any innovation at this level (5.4.1 Testing Value).

Illustration:

Let us these methods to explain simply the evolution of software and word-processing systems.

1. Innovation starts as a thought experiment so that we can quickly test the new envisioned system mentally. We do not try to work out every idea in a word-processing program. We have to think through and model it first.

2. We must identify the components parts in the situation by dividing it in time, space, and formula. We think about the software program and its sequences of commands, the arrangement on its screen, and its balance of functionality. The original designs of word-processing programs were much different than those we see today because of the force of innovation.

3. We attempt to identify components that can be eliminated entirely. Early word-processing programs required a "return" press at the end of each line like a typewriter. It was eventually realized that it was unnecessary and removed. As software programs advance by adding new features, they grow bigger, slower, and more complex to use. Over time, this creates an opportunity to eliminate the least valuable of those features and offer a product that is smaller, quicker, and simpler.

4. We attempt to identify components that are proven to work in a similar situation or function. We look at competing and other popular software products to see how they are sequenced, arranged, and balanced to get new ideas for our own.

5. We attempt to replace one existing element with an analogous alternative. While wordprocessing programs don't normally need mathematical spreadsheets in them, they do require something similar, textual information in rows and columns. In word-processing, this was originally done through complicated tabbing. These procedures are best replaced by the row and column framework on a spreadsheet.

6. We attempt to add one new element to fill an opening in the existing system. Word processing and spreadsheets were once very separate programs, but as people began to need to insert spreadsheets in their written documents, features were added to link the two.

7. Test the resulting changes to see what the effect is on the whole system. In software, we actually want to test our models by running them past users before we do the actual programming. After the programming, we have to test usability again.

7.4.0 Competitive Timing

Sun Tzu's six key methods on the role of timing in creating momentum.

A hawk suddenly strikes a bird.
Its contact alone kills the prey.
This is timing."

Sun Tzu's The Art of War 5:3:4-6

"You win battles by knowing the enemy's timing, and using a timing which the enemy does not expect."

Miyamoto Musashi

General Principle: Surprises should be revealed at the height of expectations or the height of chaos.

Situation:

The world of competition is chaotic and confusing. We uses standard methods to create expectations to give others the sense that they are in control. We unleash surprises to take away that sense of control and replace it with alternatives that we control. Since we are more prepared for the surprise than others, especially our rivals, we have more objective control. This little bit of objective control is magnified subjectively, as people compare us to our potential rivals.

We use the constant tiny shifts in our methods between standards and innovation to build up our momentum. Released gradually into our environment, those little bursts of momentum are quickly dissipated. The competitive environment is large and, on a day-to-day basis, we cannot have any real impact upon it. Our small innovations are quickly copied by others. We need something more.

Opportunity:

For potential supporters, we want to use the excitement of surprise to give them the emotional impetus that they need to make a decision in our favor. For our competitors, we want to demonstrate our momentum at the right time. This increases their confusion and decreases their confidence. Even though our momentum will always be small in the larger world, the difference between that momentum and others' expectations can be enough to tip the balance if it is introduced at the right time.

We use standard methods to navigate challenges, but we must get creative to establish new positions. Too many people defuse the power of momentum through poor timing. By introducing innovations at the wrong time or in the wrong way, we can strengthen or kill any momentum we have. We cannot release changes too soon, but we also cannot go too long without releasing them. When we release them, we must be ready to claim our position, the final step in the Listen>Aim>Move>Claim cycle. One step must follow another quickly. Momentum used correctly can wash away any obstacles that we face in establishing a position.

Key Methods:

The following six key methods describe the basic elements of good strategic timing.

1. Timing is the difference between strong moves and weak ones. The same move doesn't have the same power at different times. While surprise and innovation are always useful, their utility is magnified by having the right conditions in the environment. We use timing to leverage the chaos, complexity, and resulting confusion that defines competitive environments (3.2.1 Environmental Dominance).

2. Timing switches from standard practices to innovation and back again at the most productive times. Because the impact of surprise is only temporary, we must use it wisely. Momentum requires both standards and innovation. Just as the impact of innovation must be setup by creating expectations through standards, the gains won from innovation must be maintained by standards after the fact (7.1.3 Standards and Innovation).

3. We prepared our surprises and innovations in advance, keeping them secret. Instead of dissipating our momentum potential at the wrong time, we keep our innovations secret, hidden from the larger environment. We accumulate potential surprises over time until the time is right to use them. (2.7 Information Secrecy).

4. We wait until the right psychological moment, when confusion and chaos peak or when our opponents respond to our expected action. Either of these two situations offers us the psychology we need to leverage our surprise. When chaos and confusion dominates and reaches its height, people are psychologically vulnerable to surprise. When our opponents think they have a response prepared for our expected actions, their confidence also create a vulnerable psychological state (7.1.2 Momentum Psychology).

5. We then release our surprises in an instant. At the right moment, the faster we can make people aware of our surprise, the better. We want to focus this initial surprise on the smallest possible moment in time to create the maximum of confusions (5.5 Focused Power

6. We wait long enough for others to react, then we followup with another surprise. This is one reason we accumulate potential surprises. A single surprise only sets the table. The followup surprise wins the day. Since we know the surprise we plan, we can anticipate the reaction. We can choose our followup surprise to further undermine that reaction, completely taking control of the situation at least for that moment (7.2.2 Preparing Expectations).

Illustration:

Let us illustrate these ideas with the typical "October Surprise " used in politics, specifically in the 2008 election between Obama and McCain and the 1972 contest between Nixon and McGovern.

1. Timing is the difference between strong moves and weak ones. As every close Presidential election, an unexpected event will arise that is called an October surprise whether it is planned or not. In the last election, it was the financial crisis from Fanny, Freddy, and Goldman Sachs packaging "affordable mortgages" as high-grade investments. In 1972, it was Kissinger's announcement of "peace is at hand" in Vietnam.

2. Timing switches from standard practices to innovation and back again at the most productive time. Both in before the surprise and in reacting to it, the politician must demonstrate his standard abilities. The candidate that makes the fewest mistakes in their standard response to the surprise succeeds. In 2008, Obama handled the timing right by using it to return to his well-established "blame Bush/Republicans" theme but McCain broke down, reacting in a non-standard way, "halting" his campaign. In Nixon's case, the controlled surprise occurred after a campaign that had already given him a substantial lead. The surprise itself was designed around the central theme of Nixon's opponent, McGovern, ending an unpopular war.

3. We prepared our surprises and innovations in advance, keeping them secret. Since politicians are poor strategists, they are more often the victims of surprise than its controllers. That was certainly true in the last election. However, the first October Surprise was on October 26, 1972, when Henry Kissinger announced a breakthrough in negotiations with the N. Vietnamese on the eve of the election vote between Nixon and McGovern.

4. We wait until the right psychological moment, when confusion and chaos peak or when our opponents respond to our expected action. While the financial crisis wasn't planned, it certainly came at the right moment, when McCain was closing with Obama in the polls. In 1972, the surprise gave Nixon the momentum necessary to win by 20%.

5. We then release our surprises in an instant. In both cases, the news was unexpected and sudden.

6. We wait long enough for others to react, then we followup with another surprise. Politicians, being poor strategists, seldom have a series of surprises planned to seize the momentum at that point. In 2008, neither politician was in control and neither knew how to prepare a surprise, much less a followup. In 1972, it was simply unnecessary. Since McGovern's campaign was primarily a protest to the war in Vietnam, the "peace is at hand" announcement was the final nail in the coffin, costing him every state except Massachusetts.

7.4.1 Timing Methods

Sun Tzu's four key methods about the three simplest methods of controlling timing.

"When you fall behind, you must catch up.
When you get ahead, you must wait.
You must know the detour that most directly
accomplishes your plan."

Sun Tzu's The Art of War 7:1:11-3

"We look smarter than we probably really are, but it was good timing."

Victor Campbell

General Principle: Control people's emotions by speeding up, slowing down, or switching the timing of expected events.

Situation:

Controlled environments consist of a series of scheduled events, but most events in competitive environments occur unexpectedly. Key conditions, such as opportunities, arise out of complex inter-actions that cannot be predicted. Decision-making in controlled environments is easy because we know what to expect, and, more importantly, when to expect it. Decisions about timing in competi-tive environments are much more uncertain. We respond to the unknown emotionally. The time pressure in competitive environ-ments naturally results in frustration, tension, and fear.

Opportunity:

Though we cannot predict the flow of competitive events, we do control the timing of our own competitive actions and responses. We can use this control to impact people's emotions positively or negatively, as we choose. We know where their information is limited (2.1.1 Information Limits). Our opportunity is to work on this emotional gap. To the extent that we can influence the timing of events, we can either increase or decrease people's sense of cer-tainty and control. We use timing to give ourselves a competitive edge. In areas where others have a natural advantage because they control most of what happens in that environment, we can use the timing of responses to disrupt that advantage.

Key Methods:

The following key methods describe the goal and major methods for controlling timing in competitive environments.

1. The use of timing is primarily psychological. Our goal is to increase or decrease people's feelings of confidence and control. We use our control of timing intentionally to create a certain mental state in others that gives us more control over the situation. No matter which timing methods we use, our goal should be to positively affect our supporter and negatively impact our opponents. Unexpected timing creates a predetermined emotional reaction where the expected event creates no reaction at all (7.1.2 Momentum Psychology).

2. We can delay our actions to slowing down expected events. Slowing things down is the easiest method to affect timing. Done correctly, slowing down events can decrease our costs while increasing both the cost and frustration of opponents. We can use it intentionally to increase the tension in a situation so that we frustrate people's expectations. This creates the opportunity to relieve that tension with a surprise (4.2 Choosing Non-Action).

3. We can use our resources to speed up expected events. Speeding things up is generally harder than slowing them down, but it is a powerful tool. By speeding up events we can catch people offguard. The emotional effect can be either positive of negative. We can speed up expected events to better satisfy supporters who expect to wait. We can also speed up expected events to increase the pressure on opponents (5.3.1 Speed and Quickness).

4. We can replace an expected event with an unexpected one. Changing the expected into the unexpected demands the most creativity, but it can also be the most rewarding. Thinking ahead, we set up the expected event with the purpose of changing it at the time of our choice. We can also let others set up the expectations and then invent a way to transform the expected event into something. This works both to please those who support we want and to frustrate those who are opposing us. We come up with ideas for replacement using the normal methods of strategic creativity (7.3 Strategic Innovation).

Illustration:

Let us think about how a lawyer might use these methods to frustrate an opponent in a civil lawsuit.

1. The use of timing is primarily psychological. The purpose of controlling timing is simply to create frustration and increase legal expenses for opponents, not to win the case.

2. We can delay our actions to slowing down expected events. We can set a court date with the advanced intention of canceling it the last moment. We let our opponents prepare for that date, then at the last minute, we can call the judge and ask for the date to be moved because we came down with the flu.

3. We can use our resources to speed up expected events. We can plan a distant court date, say six months ahead of time, with the intention of changing it. While our opponents take their time getting ready, we do all the work necessary to have our case ready in three months. We then ask the court to move up the court due to a later conflict in our calendar. We can tell the judge that the opposition has already had three months to get ready.

4. We can replace an expected event with an unexpected one. We set up a deposition for one person. Then, at the last minute, that person has "unexpected" scheduling conflicts. Rather than completely cancel the deposition date, we arrange to be in another place to be deposed.

7.4.2 Momentum Timing

Sun Tzu's five key methods on the relative value of momentum at various times in a campaign.

"Your momentum is like the tension of a bent crossbow. Your timing is like the pulling of a trigger."
Sun Tzu's The Art of War 5:3:12-13

"If your position is everywhere, your momentum is zero."
Douglas Hostadter

General Principle: Momentum is more valuable at the end of a move or campaign than the beginning.

Situation:

Inertia can a) prevent us from getting going, b) slow our progress, and c) prevent us from completing a move. The momentum created by surprise is needed to overcome inertia, but that momentum fades quickly. Momentum tends to shift from one side to another. If we do not choose the right moment to try to create momentum, this work can be largely wasted. Basic methods of controlling timing are easy to use frequently, but timing surprises to change momentum is more challenging (7.4.1 Timing Methods).

Opportunity:

There are important pressure points at which momentum is most valuable. These pressure points are determined by the specific conditions of our situation. The longer a move or campaign continues, the more everyone expects it to continue along the same path, the greater its apparent inertia (7.2.2 Preparing Expectations). The better we understand the direction of that inertia, the easier it is for us to know the point at which releasing a surprise is the most valuable. The direction of inertia can only be changed by the application of a shift in momentum.

Key Methods:

The following five key methods explain the relative value of momentum at various times in a campaign.

1. The momentum needed to overcome inertia only comes from combining strategy practices with an innovation. All appropriate responses are amplified by the use of innovation creating surprise. We must use both the standard methods of strategy and know how to innovate in all those situations (7.1.3 Standards and Innovation).

2. Momentum is more valuable at the end of a move or campaign than the beginning. There are three points at which we can use momentum, the beginning, middle, or end. All of these points are not created equal. The most valuable is the momentum that gives us victory at the end. The least valuable is the momentum that gets us started in the beginning. The surprise that keeps us going in the middle is simply a necessity (6.3 Campaign Patterns).

3. If inertia prevents us from getting started, we can start our move or campaign with a surprise. This is valuable in a situation where we need to get some type of foothold to get started. However, surprises that get initial attention create the least valuable form of momentum, or, more accurately, the most over-rated. In today's world, the attempt to introduce new organizations via an attentiongetting "surprise" has become common. Unfortunately, these attempts seldom work. When such an attempt does get attention, it can get a lot of attention, which makes this method seem like a better strategy than it really is. Its weakness arises from its failure to start with standards (7.2 Standards First).

4. If inertia is slowing us, we can use surprise to make faster progress. Momentum is more valuable to get us unstuck in the middle of a campaign. We can use it to lock in our progress thus far and create more optimism about our potential success. Applied at the proper time, it can help us avoid the later, most difficult stages of a campaign (7.1.2 Momentum Psychology).

5. We use surprise toward the end of a move or campaign to overcome the final barriers that stand between us and success. Momentum that gives us victory is the most valuable because it decides the issue, getting us to the new position where our efforts can pay off. At this stage, we also have had the most time to prepare the situation, creating the expectations that in turn create the most momentum (7.2.2 Preparing Expectations).

Illustration:

Let us illustrate these key methods for the art of sales.

1. The momentum needed to overcome inertia only comes from combining strategy practices with an innovation. A sales presentation that is completely routine is completely forgettable. It might inform buyers, but it will not motivate them to decide.

2. Momentum is more valuable at the end of a move or campaign than the beginning. The goal of every sale call is to move the sale process forward, but the goal of the process is to get a decision in our favor from the buyer.

3. If inertia prevents us from getting started, we can start our move or campaign with a surprise. If, for example, we cannot even get into see the buyer, we may have to get innovative to get the appointment.

4. If inertia is slowing us, we can use surprise to make faster progress. If the sales process bogs down, prospects can easily lose interest. We can use surprise and innovation to recapture interest and create emotion to keep it moving.

5. We use surprise toward the end of a move or campaign to overcome the final barriers that stand between us and success. Emotion is required to commit to a buying decision. This means that the emotion created by a change of emotion is the most valuable at the close. The surprise should not be so disconcerting that the buyer must rethink everything, but surprising enough to create excitement.

7.4.3 Interrupting Patterns

Six key methods regarding how repetition creates patterns for surprise.

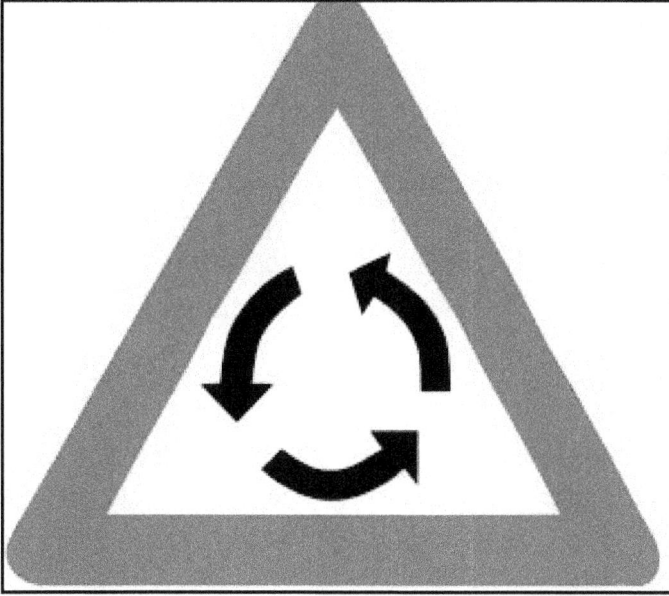

"You must force the enemy to move to your advantage. Use your position."
Sun Tzu's The Art of War 5:4:16-17

"Repetition of the same thought or physical action develops into a habit which, repeated frequently enough, becomes an automatic reflex."
Norman Vincent Peale

General Principle: Good timing requires creating and interrupting patterns of repetition.

Situation:

While a single surprising event can determine success in a given meeting over the length of a competitive campaign requires multiple surprises. The problem is that when repeated, a surprise ceases to be surprising. Because we are human, we gravitate toward patterns of behavior. We repeat what has worked in the past. We use regular cycles of specific actions at certain times in a particular order. People fall into these patterns because they are comfortable and make life easier because fewer decisions are required. People fall into these formulaic patterns even when they attempt to surprise people. Everyone who regularly watches horror movies is familiar how the "cat jumping out of closet" surprise is set-up but movie makers still use it because they know that it has worked well in the past.

Opportunity:

While repeated attempted surprises can lose their ability to create emotion, repetition can also increase the surprise if done correctly. What we are really saying is that repetition changes expectation. Whenever we create expectation, we can violate those expectations to create surprise.

These patterns of behavior make people predictable.

Key Methods:

There are six key methods for using patterns to create surprise and to build momentum.

1. The secret of timing interruptions is building pressure and releasing it at the right time and place. The breaking of a regular pattern to surprise must have an impact. We must time our surprises precisely. Released at the appropriate time, our built up momentum introduces a critical amount of control into the chaos of competition. For a period of time, it becomes a force with which we control and others must cope. It is this control that has the most to impact on others' attitudes about our position (7.4 Competitive Timing).

2. The repetition of similar events in a regular pattern is comforting because it creates expectations. By being dependable and seemingly predictable in our patterns, we win people's trust by *not* exciting them. It is that trust that moves people into position to be surprised. A regular cycle of behavior makes this easier. People move forward when they think that they know what to expect. We use patterns to make people comfortable so they can stay with us in the process and so we don't lose them. We must innovate continually but secretly. While we innovate, we uses standards to shape people's expectations so that they are not expecting anything novel or shocking (7.2.2 Preparing Expectations).

3. The repetition of contradictory events at seemingly random times creates surprise and excitement. We must time our surprises to break the pattern. Whether we have set up expectations through our patterns or they have set their own expectations through their habits, we can create a reason to interrupt that pattern. Momentum is wasted if it is released before people are ready. We prepare our surprises in advance but keep them a secret (7.1.2 Momentum Psychology).

4. Interruptions in patterns should appear random, but they should be designed to create decisions. Since people use habits to avoid making decisions, we interrupt those patterns to force decisions on them. People's decisions take place in an instant. We must make our impact at the point of decision. We must time our surprise so we release that tension in the direction that we want (6.8 Competitive Psychology).

5. We must invest only in efforts that win supporters or frustrate opponents to build our positions. We want to confuse people only in a way that gives us control. We only want to create confusion and chaos at the point at which we are ready to provide direction in the situation. A sudden shift from what is expected creates tension. We want to use that tension as the basis for building our position not increasing chaos (7.1 Order from Chaos).

6. *We use surprise to encourage others to think or act in a new way.* We use momentum to give us a brief moment when we control others. We use control of our supporters to control our competitors. We want to shape the process so both supporters and competitors rush forward without stopping, going where we want them to go. We release them only at the right time to get the decisions that we want. This requires thinking about timing and knowing exactly where we are in our moves (2.3.1 Action and Reaction).

Illustration:

Let us illustrate these key methods in the context of making a presentation.

1. *The secret of timing interruptions is building pressure and releasing it at the right time and place.* Most presentations are boring, predictable, and forgettable. We can use patterns and interruptions to create more impact in our presentations.

2. *The repetition of similar events in a regular pattern is comforting because it creates expectations*. At the beginning of a speech, we can set out the pattern, the topics to be covered and the pattern in which they are covered.

3. *The repetition of contradictory events at seemingly random times creates surprise and excitement.* After establishing a fairly boring pattern, say by showing a series of slides, we can interrupt that pattern, say by showing a slide upside down and standing on our head to give it.

4. *Interruptions in patterns should appear random, but they should be designed to create decisions*. The upside down slides should make a point, create a pattern of their own, and illustrate a decision that has to be made. For example, they could illustrate how people go out of their way to make things difficult rather than make a decision.

5. We must invest only in efforts that win supporters or frustrate opponents to build our positions. We should use this technique only to the point it is valuable for making its point and entertaining the audience, past a certain point, like any repeated device, it becomes boring and annoying.

6. We use surprise to encourage others to think or act in a new way. It isn't enough to simply have the presentation be memorable, we want it to be effective at getting the decision that we want. The point of the surprise is completing the move.

7.5.0 Momentum Limitations

Sun Tzu's six key methods on the implications of momentum's temporary nature.

> *"Surging water flows together rapidly.*
> *Its pressure washes away boulders.*
> *This is momentum."*
>
> Sun Tzu's The Art of War 5:3:1-3

> *"If you're coasting, you're either losing momentum or else you're headed downhill."*
>
> Joan Welsh

General Principle: We must translate a temporary advantage in momentum into a permanent advantage in position.

Situation:

While it takes time for positions to erode, the momentum from surprise is lost almost immediately. In Sun Tzu's division of the elements of a position, it is a temporary environmental component of a position, not a persistent one (1.4 The External Environment]). As such, momentum is never controlled by one party for very long. By definition, surprise cannot last. It quickly becomes part of the new status quo. It can not be gained and only lost by the party that has it. As with all complementary opposites, we can leverage this natural balancing of temporary and persistent elements to our advantage, but only if we understand how.

Opportunity:

Whether we have just won momentum or just lost it, we have an opportunity. Those two opportunities are very different. If an opponent currently has momentum, we have the opportunity to seize that momentum for ourselves, ideally at just the right time (7.4.2 Momentum Timing). If we currently have momentum ourselves, our job is the more complicated task of translating that temporary advantage into a more permanent aspect of our position.

Key Methods:

The following six key methods describe how we must deal with momentum's limitations in advancing our position.

1. We must react immediately to shifts of momentum. One of the foundations of strategy is the idea that all strategic positions are temporary. The temporary nature of momentum forces us to think one step ahead of the curve. We always have to be thinking about the next move in the game. Since innovation plays a role in every situation, a major part of good strategy is working these swings of momentum correctly (1.1.1 Position Dynamics).

2. When we lose momentum to an opponent, we must prepare for getting it back. Momentum switches back and forth. Only the competitor that has momentum at any given time is in a position to lose it. The most productive way to think about the loss of momentum is to see it as an opportunity to frustrate opponents by stealing their new found momentum away again (7.3.1 Expected Elements).

3. We stop opponents from converting their momentum into blocking their advance. This is only important when any advance in their position blocks us. When it does, we must stop them from making successful claims based upon their momentum. This requires knowing the specific components necessary for making a claim (8.2 Making Claims).

4. When we gain momentum in a contest, we use it to get in position to make a claim. When we have momentum, we must translate its energy into a permanent improvement in our position. In Sun Tzu's terms, this must mean we must shift from the "Move" step to the "Claim" step of the adaptive loop (1.8 Progress Cycle).

5. Translating momentum into persistent position requires gaining control of additional resources. This requires either taking control of new resources physically or subjectively leveraging the new subjective opinions of others regarding our capacities (7.5.1 Momentum Conversion).

6. When innovation is translated from momentum into position, its ability to create new momentum diminishes. This is the process by which the spread of innovation creates new standards. These new standards become part of the expectations by which comparisons are made (7.5.2 The Spread of Innovation).

Illustration:

These principles can be illustrated in any competitive arena. Let's look at some examples in sports, business, and politics.

1. We must react immediately to shifts of momentum. In any type of sporting, business, or political contest, as long as both "teams" use the expected game plan, the historically stronger team has the advantage. These expectations are destroyed when the underdog does something surprising to seize the initiative. On the field, we can actually see the psychological effects of momentum.

The team that has the momentum plays more confidently. Seizing the initiative improves their execution in tangible ways.

2. When we lose momentum to an opponent, we must prepare for getting it back. But that burst of energy and inspiration cannot last. With momentum on their side, the opponent plays with more confidence and focus, but their momentum only lasts until the opposing team is able to undermine that sense of superiority, seizing back the initiative with their own surprise.

3. We stop opponents from converting their momentum into blocking their advance. When a team loses momentum, they must focus on not making any mistakes and instead focus on technique for slowing down the play. When a company loses momentum to a competitor's announcement, they must immediately work to confuse the market by countering with their own announcements so that customers will wait to see what happens before buying. When a politician loses momentum by losing a primary in a surprising manner, he or she must avoid overreacting and further alienating voters. Instead, he or she must create a new surprise by congratulating the opponent and honestly recognizing what the opponent did better and he or she did wrong.

4. When we gain momentum in a contest, we use it to get in position to make a claim. When a team seizes momentum by making a surprising play, they must immediately do their best to score. When a company seizes the momentum by making a surprising announcement, they must immediately work on translating that announcement into sales or commitments for sales. In a political battle, the surprise, such as a win in a primary in a U.S. presidential race, should immediately be converted into broader endorsements.

5. Translating momentum into persistent position requires controlling additional resources. In a sports contest, it must be converted into a score. In business, it must be converted into sales. In politics, it must be converted into votes.

6. When innovation is translated from momentum in position, its ability to create new momentum diminishes. They create a new set of expectations about which contestant is the strongest. This brings us back to step one in this process.

7.5.1 Momentum Conversion

Sun Tzu's six key methods on converting momentum into positions with more value.

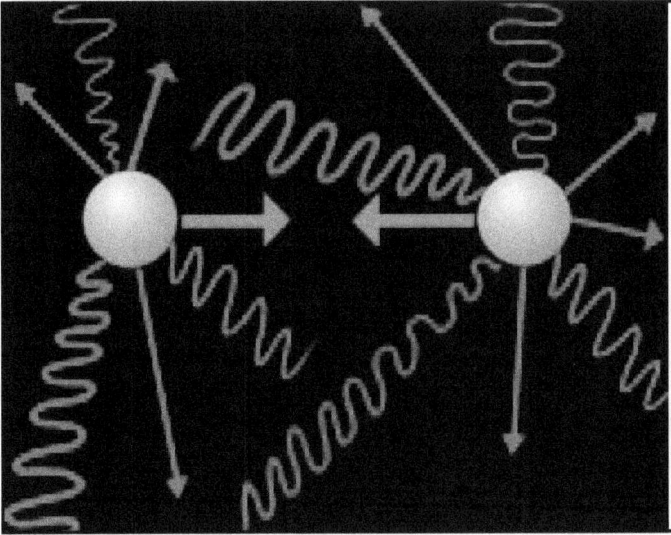

"You make your men powerful in battle with momentum. This should be like rolling round stones down over a high, steep cliff. Momentum is critical."

Sun Tzu's The Art of War 5:5:13-15

"Creativity is not the finding of a thing, but the making something out of it after it is found."

James Russell Lowell

General Principle: Momentum permanently affects a position by making our claims more successful and profitable.

Situation:

Many people don't get any benefit from their creativity. Sun Tzu sees momentum as potential energy. It needs to be converted into movement. His analogy is converting an object's potential energy into movement by rolling it downhill. People fail to see how creativity must be used as a part of the larger process. In school, many of us are taught to confuse creativity with self-expression, which is an end in itself. The solution to this confusion is creativity. Both creativity and the momentum that it can produce are only means to an end.

Opportunity:

In Sun Tzu's system, our creative opportunity is part of the larger process. Sun Tzu's strategy is a method for making decisions about changing conditions to improve positions. We use creativity to create surprise, surprise to create momentum, momentum to complete a move, and a move advances our position in a way that pays. Our opportunity is to combine innovation with standards to create surprise (7.1.3 Standards and Innovation). We combine surprise with timing to create momentum (7.4 Competitive Timing). We combine momentum with our current position to complete a move. We combine this move with economics to make our position pay.

Key Methods:

The following six key methods look at how momentum not only completes a move but makes it pay.

1. In competition, our physical positions arise from other peoples support of our position. All of our assets come from our position--the paycheck from our job, the good will in our business, social, and personal relationships, and our property and other assets. That position depends on others recognizing our rights of ownership. Without that support, we lose those assets (2.3 Personal Interactions).

2. *Temporary momentum changes people's subjective view of our position*. The momentum itself may fade, but the fact that we have been creative and surprising becomes part of our position's history. People's persistent attitudes about us factor in these abilities made visible by a momentum shift (1.2 Subobjective Positions).

3. *The momentum from surprise completes the move to setup claiming rewards*. Just like standard responses set up the expectations that surprise changes to create momentum, that momentum sets up the expectations that lead to the next element of getting rewarded, making a claim (8.2 Making Claims).

4. *Making a claim require others to make decisions about us*. This is the topic of the next section, but the basic concept is simple: we must ask for rewards in order to get them. Claims take advantage of the momentum we have created. When we complete our moves after getting momentum, other people have a different mindset about us when they make these decisions. They are much more likely to make decisions in our favor because of the new perspective created by momentum (2.3.1 Action and Reaction).

5. *This change in perception reduces our costs and amplifies our rewards for a move*. A lot goes into a making a move in Sun Tzu's system, from picking the right opportunities to knowing the right responses to the conditions we find, to creating momentum, to making claims. But the end goal is always the profitability of our move. We can use momentum to make our moves pay better than they would otherwise (3.1.2 Strategic Profitability).

6. *These rewards remain long after momentum is lost*. Despite the temporary and limited nature of momentum, the rewards that it wins are long-lasting. When we ask supporters for their support with momentum, they will give it. After people have given their support, they do not take it away unless we give them a reason to do so. In the future, opponents will treat our moves with more caution, expecting us to turn around challenges in surprising ways. The rewards we have won verifies our abilities. Others who did not witness our moves or momentum can see their effects embodied in our position (7.5 Momentum Limitations).

Illustration:

Let us illustrate these ideas by looking at how Apple leverages their innovations into sales.

1. In competition, our physical positions arise from other peoples support of our position. Apple has developed a reputation for innovation that leads others to follow it instead of attack it.

2. Temporary momentum changes people's subjective view of our position. Introduction of novel products has shaped people's perceptions of Apple. Even when their ideas are less than successful, think back to the Newton, every new innovation adds to this reputation because it has become a permanent aspect of their market position.

3. The momentum from surprise completes the move to setup claiming rewards. The recent introduction of the iPad was introduced as a market innovation that gives Apple momentum in a new segment of the market, competing with devices such as Amazon's Kindle.

4. Making a claim require others to make decisions about us. In the case of the iPad, these claims will either succeed or fail when the new device goes on sale next month. iPhone and iPod Touch users will have to decide if the new idea is valuable.

5. This change in perception reduces our costs and amplifies our rewards for a move. Because the device is creative, it gets a lot of free publicity, reducing Apple's costs of advertising, and Apple is able to charge a premium for it, increasing their rewards.

6. These rewards remain long after momentum is lost. If successful, a year of two from now the iPad will lead a new segment and as the leader reap the majority of market profits. However, even if the product fails like the Newton, it will still enhance Apple's reputation as an innovator. This brings us back to step one that made the move possible.

7.5.2 The Spread of Innovation

Sun Tzu's four key methods for using the spread of innovation to advance our position.

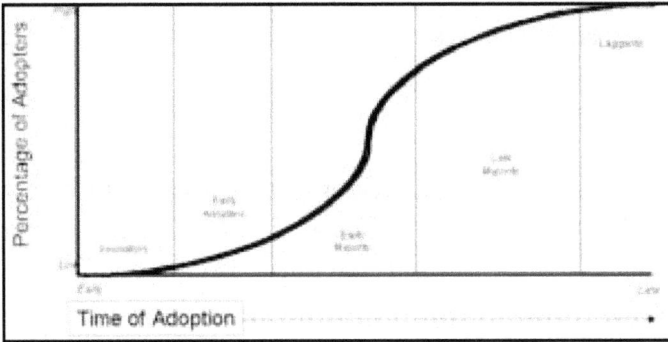

"Use your position.
The enemy must follow you.
Surrender a position.
The enemy must take it."

Sun Tzu's The Art of War 5:4:16-20

"You must not for one instant give up the effort to build new lives for yourselves. Creativity means to push open the heavy, groaning doorway to life. This is not an easy struggle. Indeed, it may be the most difficult task in the world, for opening."

Daisaku Ikeda

General Principle: Innovation spreads in a pattern that favors early adopters not inventors.

Situation:

The problem is that the competitive landscape is constantly changing in ways that most people fail to predict. While momentum from creative surprise evaporates more quickly than we expect, successful innovations spread throughout the competitive landscape much slower than we expect. Worse, that spread is not smooth and constant, but lumpy and variable. The new landscape arises gradually, not from the actions of any one player, but by the decisions by different groups of people at different times. This means that as an innovation spreads, the landscape is broken by different sets of standards at different places that are distributed in unpredictable ways.

Opportunity:

The opportunity is that, despite most people's failure to predict changes in the competitive landscape, those changes are predictable in a more general way. As Sun Tzu puts it, as people change their position, abandoning old positions, others are forced to change their positions as well. One group may adopt a position that others are abandoning, but there is an overall pattern to the march of progress that we can understand in assembling our big picture of what is happening (2.5 The Big Picture). Today, we know that innovations are adopted in a pattern that is called the S-Curve. This curve starts with a small number of innovators, then a slightly larger number of early adopters, followed by a jump up to a big number of early majority, followed by the late majority, which is followed by dwindling number of laggards.

Key Methods:

The following four key methods describe how we use the spread of innovation to advance our position.

1. Most of us perceive that new methods are adopted rapidly, but this is wrong. This viewpoint reflects the perspective of the early and late majority to which most of us belong. The *early* spread of a new method, from innovator to early adopter occurs beneath the radar. Studies show that it takes from eight to twenty years for a new method to reach critical mass and take off. After reaching critical mass, the new method seems suddenly to become common knowledge, rapidly expanding in use (1.8.3 Cycle Time).

2. In this adoption curve, the opportunity resides only in the "early adopter stage." The earlier, innovator stage is a low probability point in the curve because the vast majority of innovations are never proven to have a broader utility. The early adopter stage is proves the broader value of the innovation. Once we understand the pattern by which innovation spreads, we realize that invention itself is not as valuable as the spread of innovation made possible by the proof provided by early adopters (3.0 Identifying Opportunities).

3. We position ourselves to "ride the curve upward." We use our own creativity primarily for surprise. We cannot expect to create trends that move through society. Instead, we attempt to discover new methods after they have been proven but before they have become popular. We work to find innovation in the "early adopter" stage dramatically increasing our chances of success and leveraging the larger trend toward new methods (4.0 Leveraging Probability).

4. We gradually develop expertise in the new methods that will eventually become valuable to others. We explore new methods adopting them gradually. Given the long adoption cycle, we need not rush. We practice these new methods so that their use becomes routine. Over time, we understand these methods well just as the majority begin to adopt them. This makes us an expert in the new system just as the opening is being recognized by more and more people. This positions us on the new battlefield long before others (3.1.4 Openings).

Illustration:

Every era is ripe with examples of how the people who are the most successful are not those who develop an innovation, but the early adopters who are in the right place as the innovation reaches its broader market. Henry Ford didn't invent the automobile, interchangeable parts, nor the assembly line. He was merely the early adopter of these ideas and the first applying them to car manufacturing. Bill Gates invented neither a computer language nor an operating systems, but he was an early adopter, adapting an existing language, Basic, to a new generation of microprocessors, and, after that, an early operating systems to a new generation of personal computers. After that, he simply adapted other software products--word processing, spreadsheets, email--before they had reached their mainstream audiences.

1. Most of us perceive that new methods are adopted rapidly, but this is wrong. The first cars powered by internal combustion engines appeared in 1806. The Ford Motor Company didn't appear until almost 100 years later, 1903. The first computer was introduced in 1936. Bill Gates and the personal computer arose almost fifty years, later, in the 1980s.

2. In this adoption curve, the opportunity resides only in the "early adopter stage." For car, this stage lasted for 100 years. For computers, there were several adoption cycles: mainframes, minis, and PCs.

3. We position ourselves to "ride the curve upward." Both Ford and Gates positioned themselves by bringing mass production and mass distribution to their respective fields.

4. We gradually develop expertise in the new methods that will eventually become valuable to others. While their early leads were important, early Ford and early Microsoft made themselves valuable to customers by bringing ideas introduced by others to the mainstream market by commercializing them.

7.6.0 Productive Competition

Sun Tzu's eight key methods for using momentum to produce more resources.

"There is no limit to the ways you can win."
Sun Tzu's The Art of War 5:2:23

"Price is what you pay. Value is what you get."
Warren Buffett

General Principle: Productive competition is not a zero-sum contest because innovation creates value.

Situation:

Most people don't understand how competition produces more value. One of the most common and destructive strategic mistakes is thinking that we can only win by taking from others. Contests where the winner succeeds only at the expense of the loser are called zero-sum games. While zero-sum contests like chess exist, even in real life competition, if all competition was zero-sum, progress would be impossible. The very idea of a zero-sum world is at the root of most human suffering and individual failure. It is a worldview built on a basic misunderstanding about the nature of competition, success, and human creativity.

Opportunity:

Our opportunities come from understanding how competition produces value. What we perceive as wealth and value comes from our knowledge. If our knowledge was limited and fixed, wealth and value would also be fixed as well (1.2.1 Competitive Landscapes). Since our knowledge grows, however, it creates new forms of value. Competition, rather than destroying value, is necessary to proving value. Without competition, we cannot compare one set of ideas against another to find out which is more valuable (1.3.1 Competitive Comparison). Competition tests our mental models and out of that test, we develop better models and more wealth in the competitive landscape (2.2.2 Mental Models).

Key Methods:

These are the key methods describing how competitive innovation makes the world more productive.

1. Only our knowledge makes resources valuable. When our knowledge was limited to hunting and gathering, resources were scarce. As our knowledge has expanded, resources that were once useless have become valuable. The difference between poor countries and rich is not in their natural resources It is in the knowledge of their people in knowing which methods work best (2.1 Information Value).

2. Control of resources goes to those who can use them most productively. Stone-age people fought over their hunting grounds because their knowledge was limited, which limited their resources. Those who fought over limited resources did not inherit the earth. The world went to those who mastered new skills to create more value from new resources. Our increasing knowledge opens up new forms of value. Old knowledge is replaced over time by more productive knowledge. Individuals may cling to cherished ideas of what works, but over time, we all eventually move from what works to what works better (1.8.1 Creation and Destruction).

3. Destructive competition does not determine the control of resources over the long-term. Conflict seeks to destroy opponents' positions. This does not create more value. It is costly to both winner and loser. Greater knowledge about how to a destroy an opponent give an advantage to pure destroyers over pure producers. However, pure destroyers lose to those who combine knowledge of both production and competition. Over the long-term, the real winners are those who have more knowledge about how to use resources productively because they can apply more resources to defense, which is always less expensive than any form of direct attack (1.1.2 Defending Positions).

4. Productive competition depends on exploring new opportunities that expand our knowledge. To avoid conflict, Sun Tzu's methods required us to look for openings, that is, resources that might offer advantages that others overlooked. We explore those openings to learn their value as a way of building up our position. Exploration exposes us to new resources. The exposure gives us new ideas about how to exploit those resources. Through this process, our knowledge about what resources are available and how to use them grows throughout our lives. That knowledge has grown from generation to generation throughout human history (7.6.1 Resource Discovery).

5. Only productive competition can determine the most productive use of resources. Productive competition is different from destructive conflict. Sun Tzu's productive competition is based on the idea of building up positions, which requires getting the most value out of resources. Competition does and must create more knowledge since it compares two alternative positions through outcomes. Only such comparisons can separate the good idea from the better one. By creating new knowledge, competition creates new ways of making resources more valuable (1.3.1 Competitive Comparison).

6. *Since competition requires innovation, it leverages more value from the existing resources*. We all take what we have and do the most we can with it. In competition, we focus our creativity on creating new methods via surprise. Surprise requires first mastering best practices and then going beyond them. That innovation has the by-product of discovering new, more powerful methods of using resources. Since competition exists in a more dynamic environment than production, it results necessarily in more new ideas and separates the good ideas from the bad and the better. Creative techniques are not only critical to success in competition, but they must inevitably result in more knowledge (7.3 Strategic Innovation).

7. *Both exploration and innovation expand our knowledge of what works*. Exploring new opportunities discovers untapped natural resources. Exploring new methods gives us the tools that we need to better use those new resources. This knowledge is the basis of good decisions and responses to our immediate situation, but it is more than that. This new knowledge is the basis on which competitive positions are continually created and destroyed (2.1 Information Value).

8. *The process of productive competition continually creates entirely new forms of ground*. Hunters and gathers learn agriculture become farmers. Farmers become manufacturers. Manufacturers of a few products become manufacturers of more and better products at lower prices. At every step of this process, we discover ways to turn resources that were once useless and make them valuable. The most powerful devices that we have ever created are computers based on integrated circuits. These chips are made of silicon, common, ordinary sand. The expansion of human knowledge can actually create new forms of ground as the basis of competition Today's internet is a great example since, without it, you would not be reading this (7.6.2 Ground Creation).

Illustration:

Let us apply these key methods very simply to a person's professional sales career.

1. Only our knowledge makes resources valuable. The sales skills we have, the more valuable we are to employers because the more we can do for them.

2. Control of resources goes to those who can use them most productively. As we prove our skills by generating sales for our company, we alternatively 1) get a better sales territory from our existing employer, 2) move to a new employer who will reward us better for our sales skills, or 3) start our own organization to benefit from our sales skills more directly.

3. Destructive competition does not determine the control of resources over the long-term. While we might win a sale or two by damaging the reputations of our competitors, over the long-term, such tactics will isolate us within our industry. We will eventually be overshadowed by those who can produce sales without being seen as a threat.

4. Productive competition depends on exploring new opportunities that expand our knowledge. Ten years of sales experience is different than one year of sales experience repeated ten times. If we don't explore new areas of sales responsibility or new positions at different organizations, we cannot expand our knowledge.

5. Only productive competition can determine the most productive use of resources. We learn which sales methods work and seeing who wins which sales. We learn better techniques whether we win the sale or lose it. If we win the sale, we know our methods were better in that situation. If we lose the sale, we know that our competitors techniques were better and can copy those techniques.

6. Since competition requires innovation, it leverages more value from the existing resources. Each sales situation is unique, requiring some innovation on our part. The more we learn to personalize each sale, bringing in unique aspects of the customer's situation, the more successful we are.

7. Both exploration and innovation expand our knowledge of what works. As we get more experience, we will blend the best of our current standard sales techniques with the new sales methods that we use and those that we encounter.

8. *The process of productive competition continually creates entirely new forms of ground.* The best salespeople discover new markets and create new products to address the needs in them.

7.6.1 Resource Discovery

Sun Tzu's six rules for using innovation to create value from seemingly worthless resources.

"Manage your military position like water. Water takes every shape.
It avoids the high and moves to the low.
Your war can take any shape.
It must avoid the full and strike the empty."
Sun Tzu's The Art of War 6:8:1-5

"Things only have the value that we give them."

Moliere

General Rule: The value of resource and their limits are discovered by filling pools of needs.

Situation:

Foolish nations, organization, and businesses will continue to fight costly battles over resources that grow less and less valuable over time. "Valuable" resources are always becoming less valuable as human knowledge increases. The misconception is that wealth comes from our resources rather than our knowledge. If the only real resource is the human mind, an increasing population cannot make the world tpoorer but richer because we have more minds. This is why places like Hong Kong, with virtually no natural resources other than trained minds, are much richer per person than places such as Africa where there are many more resources but few trained minds.

Opportunity:

Everyone of us has the potential to discover valuable resources. The value of resources arises from our complex interactions with each other and our environment. Our network of minds has more knowledge, ability, and resources than any individual, so we work with one another to create value from our resources. The same vast human network also forms a complex topology of needs. We employ our resources as part of a value chain transforming our resources into products that meet those needs. That complex, adaptable chain is constantly forming and reforming itself as we find new ways to introduce new resources to generate more types of value. Since the network is infinitely complex, drawing resources from everyone in the world that flows out to everyone in the world, it contains innumerable points at which we can create more value (7.6 Productive Competition).

Sun Tzu's Rules:

These are the rules defining how new resources are discovered.

1. The endless flow of our resources fills the infinite voids of our needs. This is what Sun Tzu describes as the eternal balance of fullness and emptiness. We fill our needs with limited resources, starting with our own limited time, physical and mental capabilities. When one set of needs are filled, we become aware of a new set of needs. Those who use their resources the most wisely can generate additional resources to fill more needs. Our decisions both consume or generate value (3.2.4 Emptiness and Fullness).

2. We must attempt to conserve resources by substituting less valuable resources for more costly ones. Our incentive is to consume less expensive resources satisfying one set of needs so we can have more resources to satisfy other needs. Many of these substitutions do not work except to create surprise, but by the process of continually substituting undervalued resources for more valuable ones, we eventually discover new resources that can fill our endless pools of need (7.3.3 Creative Innovation).

3. To avoid competing for valuable resources, we must explore new areas for potential value. Competing for resources makes them more expensive so we look for areas where the value of resources are overlooked. Human knowledge is always limited. Our individual ignorance represents one boundary of human knowledge. We all can explore at the boundaries of our knowledge with the potential to make a discovery of something that will work better given our unique position (2.1.1 Information Limits).

4. Our use of undervalued resources spreads to more applications. We chart the topology of human needs by filling them like water fills a series of pools. When new resources are discovered, the flow out from them fills unforeseen shapes of needs. We copy our own success. We copy each others' success. One discovery about how to utilize an undervalued resource leads to another. Success in one area inspires new ideas in another. Knowledge is easily duplicated and enhanced by its application to new areas. Different pools of need are filled with the new resources (7.5.2 The Spread of Innovation).

5. ***As the use of undervalued resources spreads, its cost rises with its value.*** As we fill those pools of need, we discover limits of value through competition. We expand our limited knowledge by identifying new resources. As the use of those resources becomes more popular, their limitation of supply become more apparent. People start competing for them, raising their price. What was once a limitation in knowledge is magically transformed into a new resource limitation (3.1.1 Resource Limitations).

6. ***These now more costly resources channel our search for advantage in a new direction.*** The pools of need are still there when the limits of any given resource are reached. We go back to looking again for undervalued resources, starting the cycle again (1.8 Progress Cycle).

Illustration:

Let us illustrate these principles by charting the discovery of value in the internet.

1. ***The endless flow of our resources fills the infinite voids of our needs.*** Everyday, we discover new resources on the internet for filling new types of needs.

2. ***We must attempt to conserve resources by substituting less valuable resources for more costly ones.*** Each of us is looking for easier ways to address all of our needs. The Internet offers a new and seemingly endless source of new resources. We can find information, download products, and make connections with a fraction of the effort such tasks once took.

3. ***To avoid competing for valuable resources, we must explore new areas for potential value.*** While the vast majority of companies fail to find new pools of value, Amazon, eBay, Google, Facebook, and many others have found them.

4. *Our use of undervalued resources spreads to more applications*. As one of these pools is discovered, others try to add on and expand it for their own benefit. We get Amazon partners, eBay reseller, Google advertisers, Facebook applications, and on and on.

5. *As the use of undervalued resources spreads, its cost rises with its value*. Eventually, these areas become more competitive and less profitable. *These now more costly resource channels our search for advantage in a new direction*. People go on to look for the next big thing, mobile applications, video-on-demand.

7.6.2 Ground Creation

Sun Tzu's six key methods describing how we use the creation of new competitive ground to be successful.

"Water follows the shape of the land that directs its flow. Your forces follow the enemy who determines how you win."

Sun Tzu's The Art of War 6:1:1

"New discoveries in science will continue to create a thousand new frontiers for those who still would adventure."

Herbert Hoover

General Principle: Breakout innovation opens up new profitable ground for exploitation with the Progress Cycle.

Situation:

The direction of innovation flow is impossible to predict. Its opportunities are determined by shape of the landscape, but unlike the physical landscape, the competitive landscape is constantly reforming as we all constantly adjust our positions. We do not know what the innovation ultimately makes possible. We also do not know how people will react to these innovations. We also cannot see the "low spots" on the periphery of the landscape that define the potential areas where standard methods can break out in the next innovation. New competitive areas are created by the joining of two characteristics that are invisible until they meet: unfulfilled need, Sun Tzu's emptiness, and innovations potential, Sun Tzu's fullness. When these areas form, we can channel our efforts and resources into an entirely new form of opportunity.

Opportunity:

The production mindset tries to plug the holes to control the existing landscape, making it more stable. The competitive mindset uses openings to explore new competitive terrain (3.1.4 Openings). Competitive strategy destabilizes existing terrain through the use of innovation to create surprise and momentum. The flow of competitive innovation destroys the original pool from which it springs, but everyone benefits over the long run (1.8 Progress Cycle). The rules of ground creation leverage our creative momentum to take us to new positions.

Key Methods:

The following key methods describe the way in which we use the creation of new ground to create value.

1. We cannot predict the direction in which new ground will be created from breakout innovations. New ground means a new competitive arena that offers new forms of rewards. This critical limitation on our knowledge means that the direction of competition will constantly change in chaotic ways (2.1.1 Information Limits).

2. We must discover and adapt more quickly to new terrain than our competition. Since we cannot know the direction or potential of these breakouts, we must be prepared to adapt to these changes if we wish to benefit from them. If we are to be successful utilizing these changes, we must use the Progress Cycle of Listen->Aim->Move->Claim more quickly than others (1.8 Progress Cycle).

3. We must listen to be the first to discover breakout innovations opening new landscapes. We look for openings in the landscape to use them as passages to new areas of opportunity. The competitive mindset is exactly opposite of the production mindset, which seeks to plug those openings in defense of existing positions. Psychologically, the fear of loss outweighs the hope for gain, which keeps most people locked into their positions. Those with dominant positions find it especially difficult to move from them. Sun Tzu's strategy is always a philosophy of expansion that looks for new areas before our potential competitors find them (3.0 Identifying Opportunities).

4. We select opportunities that aim at breakout innovations that fit our capabilities. Not all breakout innovations have a universal impact. The world only rarely creates an internet-scale revolution that changes everything. Since a more competitive world creates an increasing wealth of novel ideas, we must know how to be selective about which breakout innovations that we pursue. The most important rule in this regard is making sure that we can get to the breakout area by traveling a minimum of distance from our current position and that its shape fits our capabilities (5.0 Minimizing Mistakes).

5. We must move to win an early position in those areas. Since these are new areas, there will be a wealth of challenges to overcome. In all new areas, we must climb the learning curve. This requires knowing how to adapt standard methods to the novel conditions in new competitive arenas (7.0 Creating Momentum).

6. We must establish visible claims in the new area and have our position attached to it. Only by claiming positions that created rewards can we sustain positions in new areas. We must initially stake small claims that are easily supported. Those positions become larger and more profitable over time as the early and late majorities discover the new area. The expansion of spac e in these new competitive areas grows our position and their rewards with a minimum of effort (8.0 Winning Rewards

Illustration:

To illustrate these principles, let us look at the series of breakout innovations that flowed from the invention of the microprocessor in 1971.

1. We cannot predict the direction in which new ground will be created from breakout innovations. No one could foresee where the microprocessor would lead when it was invented in 1971. Most people saw it only as applying to a new generation of calculators. Instead, it created a series of innovations in desktop computers, software, worldwide networking, and now mobile devices. Each of these successes laid the foundation for the following innovation. Microprocessors created for calculators, opened up the new area for personal, desktop computers. Those small computers opened up consumer software business. Software opened up the potential for computer networks. Networks opened up the potential for the internet. The internet opens up a million new areas of including on-line training from organizations such as that of the Science of Strategy Institute.

2. We must discover and adapt more quickly to new terrain than our competition. The initial pioneers got to these areas very early. Microsoft and Apple were there at the beginning of the microprocessor and have ridden each successful wave, though their timing hasn't always. Each of these pools of innovation spread from the initial breakthrough and took from eight to twenty years to move from innovation to maturity.

3. We must listen to be the first to discover breakout innovations opening new landscapes. Some of these areas proved to be large pools, opening up vast, new worlds of competition, but many may remain small for a long time. Despite companies such as Yahoo being around for a long time, neither Microsoft or Apple were very interested in Internet searches, for example, until others found the profitable point in the landscape.

4. We select opportunities that aim at breakout innovations that fit our capabilities. The founders of Microsoft and Apple were both hobbyists already involved with computers at the college level but without established positions to defend in the computer business. We see this pattern duplicated over and over. Google was started by Larry Page and Sergey Brin while the two were attending Stanford University as Ph.D. candidates. They were researching search logarithms.

5. We must move to win an early position in those areas. The companies that were successful in each new wave of invention were those that were committed to the arena before it was seen by others to be profitable. Google was first incorporated as a privately held company on September 4, 1998, with its initial public offering to follow on August 19, 2004. Today, it is the most successful company in terms of sales and stock value in the Internet arena.

6. We must establish visible claims in the new area and have our position attached to it. In all these areas of technology, there were other also-rans who had comparable technology, but none of them established the visibility and thereby the acceptance of the eventual market winners. By virtue of their visibility, they were able to create the markets that they came to dominate.

Glossary of Key Concepts

This glossary is keyed to the most common English words used in the translation of *The Art of War*. Those terms only capture the strategic concepts generally. Though translated as English nouns, verbs, adverbs, or adjectives, the Chinese characters on which they are based are totally conceptual, not parts of speech. For example, the character for conflict is translated as the noun "conflict," as the verb "fight," and as the adjective "disputed." Ancient written Chinese was a conceptual language, not a spoken one. More like mathematical terms, these concepts are primarily defined by the strict structure of their relationships with other concepts. The Chinese names shown in parentheses with the characters are primarily based on Pinyin, but we occasionally use Cantonese terms to make each term unique.

Advance (*Jeun* 進): to move into new **ground**; to expand your **position**; to move forward in a campaign; the opposite of **flee**.

Advantage, *benefit* (*Li* 利): an opportunity arising from having a better **position** relative to an **enemy**; an opening left by an **enemy**; a **strength** that matches against an **enemy's weakness**; where fullness meets emptiness; a desirable characteristic of a strategic **position**.

Aim, *vision, foresee* (*Jian* 見): **focus** on a specific **advantage**, opening, or opportunity; predicting movements of an **enemy**; a skill of a **leader** in observing **climate**.

Analysis, *plan* (*Gai* 計): a comparison of relative **position**; the examination of the five factors that define a strategic **position**; a combination of **knowledge** and **vision**; the ability to see through **deception**.

Army: see **war.**

Attack, *invade* (*Gong* 攻): a movement to new **ground**; advancing a strategic **position**; action against an **enemy** in the sense of moving into his **ground**; opposite of **defend**; does not necessarily mean **conflict.**

Bad, *ruined* (*Pi* 圮): a condition of the **ground** that makes **advance** difficult; destroyed; terrain that is broken and difficult to traverse; one of the nine situations or types of terrain.

Barricaded: see **obstacles.**

Battle (*Zhan* 戰): to challenge; to engage an **enemy;** generically, to meet a challenge; to choose a confrontation with an **enemy** at a specific time and place; to focus all your resources on a task; to establish superiority in a **position**; to challenge an **enemy** to increase **chaos;** that which is **controlled** by **surprise;** one of the four forms of **attack;** the response to a **desperate situation;** character meaning was originally "big meeting," though later took on the meaning "big weapon"; not necessarily **conflict.**

Bravery, *courage* (*Yong* 勇): the ability to face difficult choices; the character quality that deals with the changes of **CLIMATE;** courage of conviction; willingness to act on vision; one of the six characteristics of a leader.

Break, *broken, divided* (*Po* 破): to **divide** what is **complete**; the absence of a **uniting philosophy**; the opposite of <u>unity</u>.

Calculate, *count* (*Shu* 數): mathematical comparison of quantities and qualities; a measurement of **distance** or troop size.

Change, *transform* (*Bian* 變): transition from one **condition** to another; the ability to adapt to different situations; a natural characteristic of **climate**.

Chaos, *disorder* (*Juan* 亂): **conditions** that cannot be **foreseen**; the natural state of confusion arising from **battle**; one of six weaknesses of an organization; the opposite of **control**.

Claim, *position, form* (*Xing* 形): to use the **ground**; a shape or specific condition of **ground**; the **ground** that you **control**; to use the benefits of the **ground**; the formations of troops; one of the four key skills in making progress.

Climate, *heaven* (*Tian* 天): the passage of time; the realm of uncontrollable **change**; divine providence; the weather; trends that **change** over time; generally, the future; what one must **aim** at in the future; one of five key factors in **analysis;** the opposite of **ground**.

Command (*Ling* 令): to order or the act of ordering subordinates; the decisions of a **leader**; the creation of **methods**.

Competition: see <u>war.</u>

Complete: see <u>unity.</u>

Condition: see **ground**.

Confined, *surround* (*Wei* 圍): to encircle; a **situation** or **stage** in which your options are limited; the proper tactic for dealing with an **enemy** that is ten times smaller; to seal off a smaller **enemy**; the characteristic of a **stage** in which a larger **force** can be attacked by a smaller one; one of nine **situations** or **stages**.

Conflict, *fight* (*Zheng* 爭): to contend; to dispute; direct confrontation of arms with an **enemy**; highly desirable **ground** that creates disputes; one of nine types of **ground,** terrain, or stages.

Constricted, *narrow* (*Ai* 狹): a confined space or niche; one of six field positions; the limited extreme of the dimension distance; the opposite of **spread-out**.

Control, *govern* (*Chi* 治): to manage situations; to overcome disorder; the opposite of **chaos**.

Dangerous: see **serious**.

Dangers, *adverse* (Ak 阨): a condition that makes it difficult to **advance**; one of three dimensions used to evaluate advantages; the dimension with the extreme field **positions** of **entangling** and **supporting**.

Death, *desperate* (*Si* 死): to end or the end of life or efforts; an extreme situation in which the only option is **battle**; one of nine **stages** or types of **terrain**; one of five types of **spies**; opposite of **survive**.

Deception, *bluffing*, *illusion* (*Gui* 詭):
to control perceptions; to control information; to mislead an **enemy**; an attack on an opponent's **aim**; the characteristic of war that confuses perceptions.

Defend (*Shou* 守): to guard or to hold a **ground**; to remain in a **position**; the opposite of **attack**.

Detour (*Yu* 迂): the indirect or unsuspected path to a **position**; the more difficult path to **advantage**; the route that is not **direct**.

Direct, *straight* (*Jik* 直.): a straight or obvious path to a goal; opposite of **detour**.

Distance, *distant* (*Yuan* 遠): the space separating **ground**; to be remote from the current location; to occupy **positions** that are not close to one another; one of six field positions; one of the three dimensions for evaluating opportunities; the emptiness of space.

Divide, *separate* (*Fen* 分): to break apart a larger force; to separate from a larger group; the opposite of **join** and **focus**.

Double agent, *reverse* (*Fan* 反): to turn around in direction; to change a situation; to switch a person's allegiance; one of five types of spies.

Easy, *light* (*Qing* 輕): to require little effort; a **situation** that requires little effort; one of nine **stages** or types of terrain; opposite of **serious**.

Emotion, *feeling* (*Xin* 心): an unthinking reaction to **aim**, a necessary element to inspire **moves**; a component of esprit de corps; never a sufficient cause for **attack**.

Enemy, *competitor* (*Dik* 敵): one who makes the same **claim**; one with a similar **goal**; one with whom comparisons of capabilities are made.

Entangling, *hanging* (*Gua* 縣): a **position** that cannot be returned to; any **condition** that leaves no easy place to go; one of six field positions.

Evade, *avoid* (*Bi* 避): the tactic used by small competitors when facing large opponents.

Fall apart, *collapse* (*Beng* 崩): to fail to execute good decisions; to fail to use a **constricted position**; one of six weaknesses of an organization.

Fall down, *sink* (*Haam* 陷): to fail to make good decisions; to **move** from a supporting position; one of six weaknesses of organizations.

Feelings, *affection*, *love* (*Ching* 情): the bonds of relationship; the result of a shared **philosophy**; requires management.

Fight, *struggle* (Dou 鬥): to engage in **conflict**; to face difficulties.

Fire (*Huo* 火): an environmental weapon; a universal analogy for all weapons.

Flee, *retreat, northward* (*Bei* 北): to abandon a **position**; to surrender **ground**; one of six weaknesses of an **army**; opposite of **advance**.

Focus, *concentrate* (*Zhuan* 專): to bring resources together at a given time; to **unite** forces for a purpose; an attribute of having a shared **philosophy**; the opposite of *divide*.

Force (*Lei* 力): power in the simplest sense; a **group** of people bound by **unity** and **focus**; the relative balance of **strength** in opposition to **weakness**.

Foresee: see **aim**.

Fullness: see **strength**.

General: see **leader**.

Goal: see **philosophy**.

Ground, *situation, stage* (*Di* 地): the earth; a specific place; a specific condition; the place one competes; the prize of competition; one of five key factors in competitive analysis; the opposite of **climate**.

Groups, *troops* (*Dui* 隊): a number of people united under a shared **philosophy**; human resources of an organization; one of the five targets of fire attacks.

Inside, *internal* (*Nei* 內): within a **territory** or organization; an insider; one of five types of spies; opposite of *Wai*, outside.

Intersecting, *highway* (*Qu* 衢): a **situation** or **ground** that allows you to **join**; one of nine types of terrain.

Join (*Hap* 合): to unite; to make allies; to create a larger **force**; opposite of **divide**.

Knowledge, *listening* (*Zhi:* 知): to have information; the result of listening; the first step in advancing a **position**; the basis of strategy.

Lax, *loosen* (*Shii* 弛): too easygoing; lacking discipline; one of six weaknesses of an army.

Leader, *general, commander* (*Jiang* 將): the decision-maker in a competitive unit; one who **listens** and **aims**; one who manages **troops**; superior of officers and men; one of the five key factors in analysis; the conceptual opposite of fa, the established methods, which do not require decisions.

Learn, *compare* (*Xiao* 效): to evaluate the relative qualities of **enemies**.

Listen, *obey* (*Ting* 聽): to gather **knowledge**; part of **analysis**.

Listening: see **knowledge**.

Local, *countryside* (*Xiang* 鄉): the nearby **ground**; to have **knowledge** of a specific **ground**; one of five types of **spies**.

Marsh (*Ze* 澤): **ground** where footing is unstable; one of the four types of **ground**; analogy for uncertain situations.

Method: see **system**.

Mission: see **philosophy**.

Momentum, *influence* (*Shi* 勢): the **force** created by **surprise** set up by **standards**; used with **timing**.

Mountains, *hill, peak* (*Shan* 山):uneven **ground**; one of four types of **ground**; an analogy for all unequal **situations**.

Move, *march, act* (*Hang* 行): action toward a position or goal; used as a near synonym for <u>dong</u>, act.

Nation (*Guo* 國): the state; the productive part of an organization; the seat of political power; the entity that controls an **army** or competitive part of the organization.

Obstacles, *barricaded* (*Xian* 險): to have barriers; one of the three characteristics of the **ground**; one of six field positions; as a field position, opposite of **unobstructed**.

Open, *meeting, crossing* (*Jiao* 來): to share the same **ground** without conflict; to come together; a **situation** that encourages a race; one of nine **terrains** or **stages**.

Opportunity: see <u>*advantage.*</u>

Outmaneuver (*Sou* 走): to go astray; to be **forced** into a **weak position**; one of six weaknesses of an army.

Outside, *external* (*Wai* 外): not within a **territory** or **army**; one who has a different perspective; one who offers an objective view; opposite of **internal**.

Philosophy, *mission, goals* (*Tao* 道): the shared **goals** that **unite** an **army**; a system of thought; a shared viewpoint; literally "the way"; a way to work together; one of the five key factors in **analysis**.

Plateau (*Liu* 陸): a type of **ground** without defects; an analogy for any equal, solid, and certain **situation**; the best place for competition; one of the four types of **ground**.

Resources, *provisions* (*Liang* 糧): necessary supplies, most commonly food; one of the five targets of fire attacks.

Restraint: see **timing.**

Reward, *treasure, money* (_Bao_ 賞): profit; wealth; the necessary compensation for competition; a necessary ingredient for **victory**; **victory** must pay.

Scatter, *dissipating* (_San_ 散): to disperse; to lose **unity**; the pursuit of separate **goals** as opposed to a central **mission**; a situation that causes a **force** to scatter; one of nine conditions or types of terrain.

Serious, *heavy* (_Chong_ 重): any task requiring effort and skill; a **situation** where resources are running low when you are deeply committed to a campaign or heavily invested in a project; a situation where opposition within an organization mounts; one of nine **stages** or types of **terrain.**

Siege (_Gong Cheng_ 攻城): to move against entrenched positions; any movement against an **enemy's strength**; literally "strike city"; one of the four forms of attack; the least desirable form of attack.

Situation: see **ground.**

Speed, *hurry* (Sai 馳): to **move** over **ground** quickly; the ability to **advance positions** in a minimum of time; needed to take advantage of a window of opportunity**.**

Spread-out, *wide* (_Guang_ 廣): a surplus of **distance**; one of the six **ground positions**; opposite of **constricted.**

Spy, *conduit, go-between* (_Gaan_ 間): a source of information; a channel of communication; literally, an "opening between."

Stage: see **ground.**

Standard, *proper, correct* (_Jang_ 正): the expected behavior; the standard approach; proven methods; the opposite of surprise; together with **surprise** creates **momentum.**

Storehouse, *house* (_Ku_ 庫): a place where resources are stockpiled; one of the five targets for fire attacks.

Stores, *accumulate, savings* (_Ji_ 糧):resources that have been stored; any type of inventory; one of the five targets of fire attacks.

Strength,*fullness, satisfaction* (_Sat_ 壹): wealth or abundance or resources; the state of being crowded; the opposite of Xu, empty.

Supply wagons, *transport* (_Zi_ 輜): the movement of **resources** through **distance**; one of the five targets of fire attacks.

Support, *supporting* (_Zhii_ 支): to prop up; to enhance; a **ground position** that you cannot leave without losing **strength**; one of six field positions; the opposite extreme of gua, entangling.

Surprise, *unusual, strange* (_Qi_ 奇) : the unexpected; the innovative; the opposite of **standard**; together with **standards** creates **momentum**.

Surround: see **confined.**

Survive, *live, birth* (*Shaang* 生): the state of being created, started, or beginning; the state of living or surviving; a temporary condition of fullness; one of five types of spies; the opposite of **death.**

System, *method* (*Fa* 法): a set of procedures; a group of techniques; steps to accomplish a **goal**; one of the five key factors in analysis; the realm of groups who must follow procedures; the opposite of the **leader.**

Territory, *terrain*: see **ground.**

Timing, *restraint* (*Jie* 節): to withhold action until the proper time; to release tension; a companion concept to **momentum.**

Troops: see **group.**

Unity, *whole, oneness* (*Yi* 一): the characteristic of a **group** that shares a **philosophy**; the lowest number; a **group** that acts as a unit; the opposite of **divided.**

Unobstructed, *expert* (*Tong* 通): without obstacles or barriers; **ground** that allows easy movement; open to new ideas; one of six field positions; opposite of **obstructed.**

Victory, *win, winning* (*Sing* 勝): success in an endeavor; getting a reward; serving your mission; an event that produces more than it consumes; to make a profit.

War, *competition, army* (**Bing** 兵): a dynamic situation in which **positions** can be won or lost; a contest in which a **reward** can be won; the conditions under which the principles of strategy work.

Water, *river* (*Shui* 水): a fast-changing **ground**; fluid **conditions**; one of four types of **ground**; an analogy for change.

Weakness, *emptiness, need* (*Xu* 虛): the absence of people or resources; devoid of **force**; the point of **attack** for an **advantage;** a characteristic of **ground** that enables **speed;** poor; the opposite of strength.

Win, *winning*: see **victory.**

Wind, *fashion, custom* (*Feng* 風): the pressure of environmental forces.

The *Art of War Playbook* Series

There are over two-hundred and thirty articles on Sun Tzu's competitive principles in the nine volumes of the *Art of War Playbook*. Each volume covers a specific area of Sun Tzu strategy.

About the Translator and Author

Gary Gagliardi is recognized as America's leading expert on Sun Tzu's *The Art of War*. An award-winning author and business strategist, his many books on Sun Tzu's strategy have been translated around the world. He has appeared on hundreds of talk shows nationwide, providing strategic insight on the breaking news. He has trained decision makers from some of the world's most successful organizations in competitive thinking. His workshops convert Sun Tzu's many principles into a series of practical tools for handling common competitive challenges.

Gary began using Sun Tzu's competitive principles in a successful corporate career and when he started his own software company. In 1990, he wrote his first *Art of War* adaptation for his company's salespeople. By 1992, his company was on *Inc. Magazine's* list of the 500 fastest-growing privately held companies in America. He personally won the U.S. Chamber of Commerce Blue Chip Quality Award and was an Ernst and Young Entrepreneur of the Year finalist. His customers—AT&T, GE, and Motorola, among others—began inviting him to speak at their conferences. After becoming a multimillionaire when he sold his software company in 1997, he continued teaching *The Art of War* around the world.

Gary has authored several breakthrough works on *The Art of War*. Ten of his books on strategy have won book award recognition in nine different non-fiction categories.

Art of War Books by Gary Gagliardi

Gary Gagliardi's Books are Available at:

SunTzus.com
Amazon.com
BarnesAndNoble.com
Itunes.apple.com